SCHOLASTIC

studySMART

Grammar Builder

Level 4
English

For information regarding permission, write to:
Scholastic Education International (Singapore) Pte Ltd
81 Ubi Avenue 4, #02-28 UB.ONE, Singapore 408830
Email: education@scholastic.com.sg

For sales enquiries write to:
Latin America, Caribbean, Europe (except UK), Middle East and Africa
Scholastic International
557 Broadway, New York, NY 10012, USA
Email: intlschool@scholastic.com

Philippines
Scholastic Philippines
Penthouse 1, Prestige Tower, F. Ortigas Jr. Road,
Ortigas Center, Pasig City 1605
Email: educteam@scholastic.com.ph

Asia (excluding India and Philippines)
Scholastic Asia
Plaza First Nationwide, 161, Jalan Tun H S Lee,
50000 Kuala Lumpur, Wilayah Persekutuan Kuala Lumpur, Malaysia
Email: international@scholastic.com

Rest of the World
Scholastic Education International (Singapore) Pte Ltd
81 Ubi Avenue 4 #02-28 UB.ONE Singapore 408830
Email: education@scholastic.com.sg

Australia
Scholastic Australia Pty Ltd
PO Box 579, Gosford, NSW 2250
Email: scholastic_education@scholastic.com.au

New Zealand
Scholastic New Zealand Ltd
Private Bag 94407, Botany, Auckland 2163
Email: orders@scholastic.co.nz

India
Scholastic India Pvt. Ltd.
A-27, Ground Floor, Bharti Sigma Centre,
Infocity-1, Sector 34, Gurgaon (Haryana) 122001, India
Email: education@scholastic.co.in

Visit our website: www.scholastic.co.in

First edition 2013
Reprinted 2015, 2016 (twice), 2018

ISBN 978-981-07-5259-0

Welcome to studySMART !

SCHOLASTIC

Grammar Builder lets your child review and apply essential grammar rules.

Knowledge of grammar is essential in ensuring your child understands the patterns and rules in the English language. As your child progresses through the practice worksheets, he will strengthen the skills needed to read and write well.

Grammar items covered in one level are reinforced at the subsequent level. This helps to ensure that your child consolidates his learning of a particular grammar item and builds upon it.

Each grammar item is covered in three pages. The first two pages target your child's ability to identify and apply the grammar item. The third page provides a quick assessment of your child's understanding of the use of the grammar item. A revision section at the end of the book also allows for easy assessment of your child's understanding of the grammar items covered in each workbook.

How to use this book?

1. Introduce the target grammar item at the top of the page to your child.

2. Direct your child's attention to the grammar box to review the grammar rule.

3. Let your child complete the practices independently.

4. Use the Assessment pages and Revision section to evaluate your child's understanding of the grammar items.

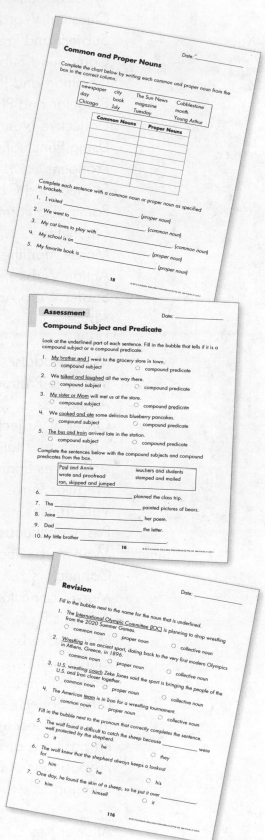

© 2013 Scholastic Education International (S) Pte Ltd   ISBN 978-981-07-5259-0

Contents

© 2013 Scholastic Education International (S) Pte Ltd ISBN 978-981-07-5259-0

Types of Sentences

A **declarative** **sentence** makes a statement. An **interrogative** **sentence** asks a question. An **exclamatory** **sentence** shows strong feeling. An **imperative** **sentence** makes a command.

What kind of sentence is each of the following? Write *declarative*, *interrogative*, *exclamatory* or *imperative* on the line.

1. Merlin carried the baby to safety.   _____D_____

2. Why did the traitors poison the town's wells?   _____In_____

3. Go back and fetch the missing sword.   _____Im_____

4. Slip the sword into the groove and pull it out.   _____Im_____

5. The king was England's bravest ruler!   _____E_____

Identify which groups of words are incomplete sentences and which are complete sentences. Write *incomplete* or *complete* on the line.

6. Sarah ^{was} at the end of the square.   _____I_____

7. The knights fought so bravely!   _____C_____

8. How did Kay treat her dog?   _____C_____

9. ^{Slip} The sword out of the stone.   _____I_____

Correct the incomplete sentences in the previous section. Add an action verb to each one. Then, rewrite the complete sentence on the line.

10. ___was_____

11. ___Slip_____

© 2013 Scholastic Education International (S) Pte Ltd ISBN 978-981-07-5259-0

Types of Sentences

Add the correct end punctuation mark to each sentence.

1. How do turtles protect themselves <u>   ?   </u>

2. What heavy, hot suits of steel they wore <u> ? ! </u>

3. Pretend that you are an acrobat or juggler <u>   .   </u>

4. The students sang songs, told stories and recited poems <u>   .   </u>

Complete each sentence with an action verb from the box below. Then, write *declarative*, *interrogative*, *exclamatory* or *imperative* on the line.

pass	won	listened	play

5. The audience <u>listened</u> to the bagpipers. <u>   D   </u>

6. What kind of games did they like to <u>play</u> ? <u> In </u>

7. Please <u>pass</u> me the pepper. <u> Im </u>

8. I've <u>won</u> three chess games in a row. <u>   D   </u>

Write an example of a declarative, interrogative, exclamatory and imperative sentence. Be sure to use the correct end punctuation.

9. declarative: <u>I robbed the bank. ✓</u>

10. interrogative: <u>Did you steal 2000 Rs. ? ✓</u>

11. exclamatory: <u>How dare you! ✓</u>

12. imperative: <u>Kill merlin. ☺ ✓</u>

6

Assessment

Types of Sentences

Decide if there is an error in the underlined part of the sentence. Fill in the bubble next to the correct answer.

1. <u>you do like</u> to see movies about knights and castles?

   ○ You do like
   ◉ Do you like
   ○ correct as is

2. Please hand me that book about the <u>Middle Ages?</u>

   ○ Middle Ages!
   ◉ Middle Ages.
   ○ correct as is

3. Grandfather described life in the early part <u>of the century.</u>

   ○ of the century?
   ○ of the century!
   ◉ correct as is

4. Why don't you write about <u>your life!</u>

   ◉ your life?
   ○ your life.
   ○ correct as is

5. <u>Begin by describing</u> your very first memory.

   ○ begin by describing
   ○ By describing
   ◉ correct as is

6. I had such fun swimming <u>in the ocean?</u>

   ○ in the ocean
   ◉ in the ocean!
   ○ correct as is

7. What do you remember about your first day <u>in school?</u>

   ○ in school!
   ○ in school.
   ◉ correct as is

8. <u>Another story</u> about our relatives in Mexico.

   ◉ Tell me another story
   ○ another story
   ○ correct as is

9. The fish looked so colorful swimming in <u>the sea.</u>

   ◉ the sea.
   ○ the sea?
   ○ correct as is

10. He told us about <u>his trip?</u>

    ○ his trip
    ◉ his trip.
    ○ correct as is

Question Words

> We use **question words** to begin questions about people (**who**, **whose**), things (**what**), places (**where**) and time (**when**).

Underline the correct question word in each question.

1. (Who / <u>Where</u>) did you go yesterday?
    I went to the beach.

2. (<u>Who</u> / What) took you there?
    My parents took me there.

3. (What / <u>When</u>) did you arrive?
    We arrived at 10 in the morning.

4. (<u>What</u> / Who) did you do when you were there?
    We cycled along the beach and had a picnic.

5. (Who / <u>Whose</u>) bicycles did you ride?
    We rode Uncle Jim's bicycles.

Complete each question with a question word.

6. _____When_____ did the storm start?
    It started soon after our
    picnic lunch.

7. _____Where_____ did you take cover?
    We took cover at a nearby café.

8. _____Who_____ did you
    meet there?
    We met our neighbors there.

9. _____What_____ happened
    after that?
    We had coffee and hot chocolate.

10. _____When_____ did you leave
    the café?
    We left after the rain stopped.

© 2013 Scholastic Education International (S) Pte Ltd ISBN 978-981-07-5259-0

Date: _____

Question Words

> We also use **question words** to begin questions about choices (**which**), reasons (**why**) or ways things are done (**how**).

Same as before

Underline the correct question word in each question.

1. (Why / Which / How) book did you buy?
    I bought the thicker one.

2. (Why / Which / How) did you choose that book?
    It had more pictures in it.

3. (Why / Which / How) pencil did you buy?
    I bought the one that had the softer lead.

4. (Why / Which / How) did you know it had a softer lead?
    I tested the pencils on a piece of paper.

5. (Why / Which / How) do you need a pencil with a softer lead?
    It is better for drawing with.

Write a question with the given question word to match each answer.

6. Which _box did you buy._____?
    I bought the pink box.

7. Why _did you buy the pink box_____?
    It's for my sister. She likes pink.

8. What _is the box for_____?
    She is going to put her toys in the box.

9. Where _will she put the box_____?
    She will put the box in her bedroom.

© 2013 Scholastic Education International (S) Pte Ltd ISBN 978-981-07-5259-0

Date: _____

Question Words

Complete each sentence. Fill in the bubble next to the correct question word.

1. __Where__ are you going in such a hurry? To the cinema.

   ○ Why
   ● Where ✓
   ○ What

2. __What__ movie are you going to watch? *The Hobbit.*

   ○ Why
   ○ Where ✓
   ● What

3. __when__ does it start? In half an hour.

   ● When
   ○ Where ✓
   ○ What

4. __who__ are you going with? Su Lin and Steve.

   ○ Why
   ● Who ✓
   ○ Which

5. __How__ are you getting there? By bus.

   ○ Why
   ○ When ✓
   ● How

6. __Which__ bus will you take, 16 or 20? 16.

   ○ Why
   ● Which ✓
   ○ How

7. __whose__ umbrella is that? Yours.

   ○ Who ✓
   ● Whose
   ○ What

8. __why__ are you still here? I'm waiting for my friend.

   ● Why
   ○ Where ✓
   ○ What

© 2013 Scholastic Education International (S) Pte Ltd ISBN 978-981-07-5259-0

Date: _____

Subject and Predicate

With mama

> The **simple subject** is the main noun that tells who or what the sentence is about. The **complete subject** is the simple subject and all the words that go with it. The **simple predicate** is the main verb. The **complete predicate** is the verb and all the words that tell what the subject does or is.

Read each sentence. Underline the complete subject and circle the simple subject.

1. A small family lived on a faraway planet.
2. The two children played near the space launch.
3. The little girl dreamed about life on Earth.
4. Huge spaceships landed daily on the planet.
5. The spaceship mechanics repaired huge cargo ships.
6. Twinkling stars appeared in the black sky.

Read each sentence. Underline the complete predicate and circle the simple predicate.

7. The planet's inhabitants lived underground.
8. A special machine manufactures air inside their homes.
9. The athletic girl jumped into the air.
10. Many toys and games cluttered the playroom.
11. The children's father described the weather.

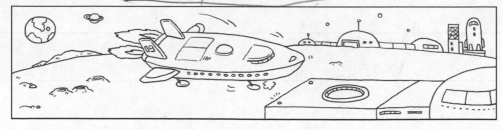

© 2013 Scholastic Education International (S) Pte Ltd ISBN 978-981-07-5259-0

Date: _____

Subject and Predicate

Draw a line between the complete subject and the complete predicate.

1. We | watched the space shuttle on TV this morning.

2. The huge spaceship | rocketed into space at 6:00 a.m.

3. During the flight, the six astronauts | released a satellite into space.

4. The space shuttle *Columbia* | circled Earth for three days.

5. The spacecraft | landed smoothly on Monday.

6. The astronauts | came back to a hero's welcome.

Write four sentences. Then, draw a line between the complete subject and the complete predicate in each sentence.

7. Ishan | loves to play with superheroes.

8. Daddy | works for the State of Maryland.

9. The lovely children | are always sweet.

10. During childhood, Mama | played with dolls.

Assessment

Date: _____

Subject and Predicate

Which part of the sentence is underlined? Fill in the bubble next to the correct answer.

1. <u>My cousin</u> lives on a big ranch in Montana.

   - ● simple subject
   - ○ complete subject
   - ○ simple predicate

2. Her family <u>raises cattle on the ranch</u>.

   - ○ simple subject
   - ● complete predicate
   - ○ simple predicate

3. Rosa's <u>job</u> is feeding the chickens before school.

   - ● simple subject
   - ○ complete subject
   - ○ simple predicate

4. Her brother John <u>feeds the horses</u>.

   - ○ simple subject
   - ○ simple predicate
   - ● complete predicate

5. <u>My cousin Rosa</u> rides her horse across this range.

   - ○ simple subject
   - ● complete subject
   - ○ complete predicate

6. John <u>spreads</u> fresh hay in the pasture.

   - ○ simple subject
   - ● simple predicate
   - ○ complete predicate

7. Their <u>neighbors</u> often go into town with them.

   - ● simple subject
   - ○ simple predicate
   - ○ complete predicate

8. The dinner bell <u>rings</u> at 6:30 every evening.

   - ○ simple subject
   - ○ complete subject
   - ● simple predicate

9. <u>The whole family</u> sits on the porch to talk.

   - ○ simple subject
   - ● complete subject
   - ○ simple predicate

10. Rosa <u>searches the Internet for sites about animals</u>.

    - ○ simple subject
    - ● complete predicate
    - ○ simple predicate

Compound Subject and Predicate

> A **compound subject** is two or more nouns connected by **and** or **or**.
> A **compound predicate** is two or more verbs connected by **and** or **or**.

Underline the nouns that form each compound subject. Then, circle the word that connects the nouns.

1. Laura and Ramona are popular story characters.

2. In one story, Pa, Ma and Laura traveled far.

3. The dog and horses trotted along.

4. Ma and Pa drove the wagon all day.

5. There were hardly any trees or bushes around.

Underline the verbs that form each compound predicate. Then, circle the word that connects the verbs.

6. The wagon swayed and creaked.

7. Laura hummed and sang.

8. The road twisted and turned.

9. Pet and Patty neighed and snorted.

10. The deer stopped and stared.

Complete the sentences with nouns or verbs joined by *and*.

11. The ___bird and the girl___ sang all day.

12. The dog ___and the cot ran___ all the way home.

© 2013 Scholastic Education International (S) Pte Ltd ISBN 978-981-07-5259-0

Compound Subject and Predicate

Underline the compound subject or the compound predicate in each sentence.
Write *CS* above each compound subject and *CP* above each
compound predicate.

1. Mike and Jody moved away.

2. They often call or e-mail us.

3. Mike jogs and swims every day.

4. Phil and Jan will visit them.

5. Juan and Yoshi moved here from other countries.

6. They speak and read English very well.

7. Lori, Sam and Beth wrote a play about moving house.

8. They practiced and presented it to the class.

9. We clapped and smiled at the end.

10. The parents and teachers liked the play.

Complete one sentence with the compound subject and the other sentence with
the compound predicate from the box.

| My dad and sister   barked and jumped |

11. Buster _barked and jumped_ when we got home.

12. _My dad and sister_ played word games for an hour.

Date: _____

Compound Subject and Predicate

Look at the underlined part of each sentence. Fill in the bubble that tells if it is a compound subject or a compound predicate.

1. <u>My brother and I</u> went to the grocery store in town.
   - ● compound subject   ○ compound predicate

2. We <u>talked and laughed</u> all the way there.
   - ○ compound subject   ● compound predicate

3. <u>My sister or Mom</u> will met us at the store.
   - ● compound subject   ○ compound predicate

4. We <u>cooked and ate</u> some delicious blueberry pancakes.
   - ○ compound subject   ● compound predicate

5. <u>The bus and train</u> arrived late in the station.
   - ● compound subject   ○ compound predicate

Complete the sentences below with the compound subjects and compound predicates from the box.

Paul and Annie	teachers and students
wrote and proofread	stamped and mailed
ran, skipped and jumped	

6. ___Paul and Annie___ planned the class trip.

7. The ___teachers and students___ painted pictures of bears.

8. Jane ___wrote and proofread___ her poem.

9. Dad ___stamped and mailed___ the letter.

10. My little brother ___ran, skipped and jumped___.

Common and Proper Nouns

> A **common noun** names any person, place or thing. A **proper noun** names a particular person, place or thing. A proper noun begins with a capital letter.

Read each sentence. Underline the common nouns. Circle the proper nouns.

1. The farmer lives in the green house down the road. ✓

2. His name is John Timus. ✓

3. The farm is next to Rising J Horse Ranch. ✓

4. Mr Timus grows wheat, soybeans and corn. ✓

5. The fields are plowed before he plants the crops. ✓

6. Mr Timus plants the crops in rows. ✓

7. As the plants grow, Mr Timus removes the weeds and looks for bugs. ✓

8. Every October, people visit the Timus Farm for the annual Harvest Celebration. ✓

Rewrite each sentence. Replace each underlined common noun with a proper noun.

9. We walked down the street to the park. ✓

   We walked down Ridge street to Central park

10. My aunt lives in the city. ✓

   My auntie Christine lives in Antwerp city.

Common and Proper Nouns

Complete the chart below by writing each common and proper noun from the box in the correct column.

newspaper	city	The Sun News	Cobblestone
day	book	magazine	month
Chicago	July	Tuesday	Young Arthur

Common Nouns	Proper Nouns
Month	Young Arthur
day	Chicago
city	Cobblestone
book	Tuesday
day	The sun news
newspaper	July
magazine	

Complete each sentence with a common noun or proper noun as specified in brackets.

1. I visited _____Ishan_____. (*proper noun*)

2. We went to _____a farm_____. (*common noun*)

3. My cat loves to play with _____yarns_____. (*common noun*)

4. My school is on _____Tuesday_____. (*proper noun*)

5. My favorite book is _____Dog man_____. (*proper noun*)

© 2013 Scholastic Education International (S) Pte Ltd ISBN 978-981-07-5259-0

Date: _____

Common and Proper Nouns

Rewrite each sentence correctly.

1. I go to stanfordshire elementary school.

   I go to Stanfordshire Elementary School ✓

2. I brought a Peanut Butter sandwich.

   I brought a peanut butter sandwich. ✓

3. We sang "somewhere over the rainbow" today.

   We sang "Somewhere over the rainbow" today ✓

4. My school is located at the intersection of maple avenue and elm street.

   My school is located at the intersection of Maple Avenue and Elm Street.

5. My best friend john sits in the third row.

   My best friend John sits in the third row ✓

6. My favorite Singer is tina bell.

   My favourite singer is Tina Bell. ✓

7. I wrote a report about Beijing in china.

   I wrote a report about Beijing in China. ✓

8. I did research on the great wall of china.

   I did research on The Great Wall of China ? ✓

Singular and Plural Nouns

A **singular noun** names one person, place, thing or idea. A **plural noun** names more than one. We add **-s** to form the plural of most nouns, except for irregular plural nouns.

Underline the singular nouns and circle the plural nouns in each sentence.

1. I opened the door and found the shoes, cap and bat I needed for the game.

2. I headed down to the field with my bat on my shoulder.

3. My friends were standing by the fence.

4. I like to play baseball with my friends.

5. My uncles taught me to stand with my feet close together.

6. I gripped the bat with my hands.

7. I hit the ball hard and ran past all the bases.

8. My team played very well that day.

Complete the sentences with the correct plural form of the noun in brackets.

9. I enjoy writing ___stories___ (story).

10. I like tales of knights and ___princesses___ (princess).

11. I also write about ___monsters___ (monster) and pirates.

12. My teacher reads my stories to many of his ___classes___ (class).

Singular and Plural Nouns

> Some nouns keep the same spelling in the singular and plural forms.

Complete the chart of irregular nouns below.

	Singular Nouns	**Plural Nouns**
1.	mouse	two mice
2.	man	men
3.	child	children
4.	tooth	teeth
5.	foot	feet
6.	ox	oxes
7.	goose	geese
8.	deer	deer
9.	sheep	sheep
10.	person	people

Complete the sentences with the plural form of the noun in brackets.

11. Those ___people___ (person) there are making too much noise.

12. They might wake up all the ___children___ (child).

13. This little boy lost his two front ___teeth___ (tooth) last week.

14. His sister could scarcely stand on her ___feet___ (foot).

15. They like to listen to me tell them ___stories___ (story).

Date: _____

Singular and Plural Nouns

Complete the paragraph with the correct form of the nouns in brackets.

I read seven 1. _____chapters_____ (chapter) of my book last night. In
chapter one, a father and his two 2. _____sons_____ (son) went to the
mountain. They built a campsite under some 3. _____trees_____ (tree)
near a creek.

The first night, the father saw a bear eating some 4. _____nuts_____
(nut). There were two bear 5. _____cubs_____ (cub) hiding in the
6. _____bushes_____ (bush). The mother bear gave the cubs
7. _____berries_____ (berry).

In the morning, they saw four 8. _____deers_____ (deer) and two
9. _____foxes_____ (fox) nearby. As they ran after them, one of the
boys fell and broke a 10. _____teeth_____ (tooth).

© 2013 Scholastic Education International (S) Pte Ltd ISBN 978-981-07-5259-0

Collective Nouns

| **Collective nouns** refer to a group of people, things or animals. |

In each sentence, circle the collective noun and underline the people, things or animals that are grouped. The first one is done for you.

1. Mom came in with a (bunch) of <u>flowers</u>.

2. She put it on top of the (chest) of <u>drawers</u>.

3. She wore a (string) of <u>beads</u> around her neck.

4. There was a (pile) of <u>clean laundry</u> on the sofa.

5. Tabby was in the corner with her new (litter) of <u>kittens</u>.

6. I was looking through my (collection) of <u>stamps</u>.

7. I had a (stack) of <u>stamp albums</u> with me.

8. Dad was cheering for his favorite (team) of <u>players</u> on television.

9. There was a large (crowd) of <u>spectators</u> at the stadium.

10. We did not (notice) the <u>swarm</u> of insects out in the garden.

Complete each sentence using one of the collective nouns above.

11. Mr Woods placed a ___bunch___ of papers in his bag.

12. He took the ___pile___ of keys from the table.

13. He looked around the room to admire his ___collection___ of pictures on the walls.

14. His favorite was the picture of a lioness with her ___litter___ of cubs.

15. A ___team___ of reporters waited for him outside his office.

Collective Nouns

> We use different collective nouns to group different things.

Circle the correct collective noun to complete each sentence.

1. When we entered the animal park, a (herd / (gaggle)) of geese greeted us.
2. Behind them, near the barn, sat a ((clutch) / brood) of chickens.
3. A (nest / (troop)) of monkeys played among the trees.
4. The tram rolled past a (troop / (herd)) of cattle.
5. Overhead, a (swarm / (flock)) of birds flew in formation.
6. Everywhere in the park, we saw ((swarms) / flocks) of tiny insects.
7. Annie yelped when she saw the (litter / (nest)) of ants.
8. She was delighted to see the ((litter) / herd) of tiger cubs.

Complete each sentence with the correct noun that is grouped. Write it on the line.

9. Farmer Tim brought us a fresh clutch of ~~milk~~ __eggs__ this morning.
    (milk / eggs)

10. Mom is baking a new batch of banana __breads__ now. (bread / eggs)

11. She bought a comb of __apples__ from the market this morning.
    (apples / bananas)

12. She has also washed a bunch of ~~flowers~~ __grapes__ for dessert.
    (flowers / grapes)

13. There is a lovely bouquet of __flowers__ on the dining table.
    (flowers / plates)

14. I am laying the table with our new shiny set of __cutlery__.
    (cutlery / napkins)

Assessment

Collective Nouns

Read each sentence. Fill in the bubble next to the collective noun.

Date: _____

1. The basketball team arrived on time.
   ○ basketball   ● team   ○ time

2. A fleet of cars were waiting for the basketball stars.
   ○ basketball   ● fleet   ○ cars

3. The stars climbed down the (flight) of stairs from the airplane.
   ● flight   ○ stairs   ○ airplane

4. The crowd of supporters cheered loudly as the stars appeared.
   ● crowd   ○ supporters   ○ stars

5. The band of musicians started playing a catchy tune.
   ○ tune   ○ musicians   ● band

Fill in the bubble next to the collective noun that correctly completes each sentence.

6. Detective Jones walked towards the __set__ of bushes.
   ○ flight   ● clump   ● set

7. He stopped at the __pile__ of clothes on the ground.
   ○ batch   ○ nest   ● pile

8. He noticed a __crate__ of empty bottles next to the clothes.
   ● crate   ○ pack   ○ clutch

9. He reached into his pocket and pulled out a __collection__ of notes.
   ● collection   ○ wad   ○ chest

10. Out of his pocket fell a __pack__ of cards.
    ● pack   ○ flock   ○ bale

© 2013 Scholastic Education International (S) Pte Ltd   ISBN 978-981-07-5259-0

Using Punctuation

> **Quotation marks** show the exact words of a speaker. When the speaker comes first, place a comma between it and the beginning of the quotation marks. When a quotation comes first, use a comma, question mark or exclamation mark before the end of the quotation marks.

Add quotation marks to show the speaker's exact words in each sentence.

1. "I have a strange case," said Mr Brown.

2. "What's strange about it?" asked Jet.

3. "Mr Hunt found an elephant," said Mr Brown.

4. "It simply appeared in his window," said Mr Brown.

5. "He must have fainted!" exclaimed Jet.

6. "No, he bought it," said Mr Brown.

Add the correct punctuation to the sentences below.

7. "What shall we do this afternoon?" asked James

8. Peter replied, "Shall we go fishing"

9. "Fishing is boring," exclaimed James

10. "Let's go skating instead," said Ian

11. "Mum, may we go out today," asked the boys.

12. Mum said, "Only after you finish your work"

26

Using Punctuation

We use **commas** between
- the day and year in a date,
- the city and state in a location and
- a series of items except before the word **and**.

Add commas where they are needed in each sentence.

1. Mrs Wu's bank is at 92 Maple Avenue, Texas.

2. She opened an account there on August 8, 2012.

3. She also goes to the branch in Lakewood, Texas.

4. That branch opens on weekdays, Saturdays and some evenings.

5. The main office is closed on Saturdays, Sundays and holidays.

6. She saw Adam, Joan and Miss Clark at the bank.

Rewrite each sentence with the correct punctuation.

7. She asked Where would you like me to put this?

   She asked, "Where would like me to put this?"

8. You can put it on the table replied Jon.

   "You can put on the table," replied Jon.

9. Please leave the carrots onions potatoes and eggs in the fridge said Jon.

   "Please leave the carrots, onions, potatoes and eggs in the fridge," said Jon.

10. Then, send these to 12 Marsh Cross Alabama said Mr Jones.

    "Then, send these to 12 Marsh cross, Alabama", said Mr. Jones.

Assessment

Using Punctuation

Rewrite each sentence with the correct punctuation.

1. Patty asked,What book did you all read

   Patty asked,"what book did you all read"?

2. We read a book called *At the Zoo* said Mark

   "We read a book called At the zoo," said Mark.

3. It had pictures of a lion, monkeys and bears added Brent

   "It had pictures of a lion, monkeys and bears," added Brent

4. It was fascinating said Mark

   "It was fascinating," said Mark.

5. Can we go to the animal show asked Ben

   "Can we go to the animal show?" said Ben?

6. Where is the show going to be asked Patty

   "Where is the show going to be?" asked Patty.

7. The show will be at the Montry Zoo said Ben

   "The show will be at the montry zoo," said Ben.

Pronouns

> We use **interrogative pronouns** to ask questions about people (***who***, ***whose***, ***whom***) and things (***what***, ***which***). Sometimes, we use ***which*** for people as well.

Underline the correct interrogative pronoun to complete each question.

1. (<u>Who</u> / Whose) is that person next to you in the picture?
    That person is my art teacher.

2. (Which / <u>What</u>) is she doing here?
    She is helping me to paint.

3. (Who / <u>Whose</u>) brushes are you using to paint?
    I am using Siew Lin's brushes.

4. (<u>Which</u> / Who) of these paintings do you like better?
    I like the one of the horse better.

5. (Who / <u>Whom</u>) are you giving the painting to?
    I'm giving it to my mother.

Complete each question with the given interrogative pronoun.

6. What ___are you doing here___?
    I am trying to repair the toy car.

7. Whose ___toy car is it___?
    It's my brother's toy car.

8. Which ___brother are you talking about___?
    I am talking about my younger brother.

9. Who ___bought it for him___?
    My elder brother bought it for him.

Pronouns

Demonstrative pronouns, such as *this* and *these*, refer to things, places or people that are near us. Demonstrative pronouns, such as *that* and *those*, refer to things, places or people that are further away from us.

Underline the demonstrative pronoun in each sentence.

1. "This is the best cupcake I've ever had!" Sam declared.

2. "That is only because you have not tried my Mom's yet," said Ron.

3. "After tasting her cupcakes, you will not like these here," he added.

4. "Really? When can I try one of those?" asked Sam.

Complete each sentence with the correct demonstrative pronoun.

5. Raju stretched to reach a book on the top shelf and said, "I can't reach __that__."

6. A librarian brought it down for him and asked, "Is __this__ what you wanted?"

7. Raju thanked her and asked, "Are __these__ all the books you have on dinosaurs?"

8. She replied, "__these__ here are the storybooks on dinosaurs."

9. She pointed to the books at the other end of the room and said, "__those__ are non-fiction titles on dinosaurs."

10. "Then, __that__ is where I should be looking," said Raju, walking towards those shelves.

11. "__That__ was a helpful librarian," Raju said to himself.

12. "She is more helpful than all __those__ I've met before in this library," he thought.

© 2013 Scholastic Education International (S) Pte Ltd ISBN 978-981-07-5259-0

Assessment

Pronouns

Read each sentence. Fill in the bubble next to the correct interrogative pronoun.

1. _____ is this on the floor? A book.
   - ○ Who   ● What   ○ Which

2. _____ put it there? One of the boys.
   - ● Who   ○ Whose   ○ Which

3. _____ of the boys was in this room earlier? John.
   - ○ Who   ○ Whose   ● Which

4. _____ is the title of that book? *My Best Friend*.
   - ○ Who   ● What   ○ Which

5. _____ do you think the author was writing about? His dog.
   - ● Who   ○ Which   ○ Whose

Read each sentence. Fill in the bubble next to the correct demonstrative pronoun.

6. Denise held up a blouse and asked, "Mum, what do you think of _____?"
   - ● this   ○ that   ○ those

7. Mum said, "You were looking for a pink blouse. _____ is red."
   - ○ those   ○ these   ● this

8. "Look at _____ over at that rack. They are all pink," Mum added.
   - ○ this   ○ these   ● those

9. "I know, but I like this design better than _____ of the pink ones," Denise said.
   - ● this   ● that   ○ these

10. "Come over here! I think _____ are nicer, and they are pink too," Mom called out from the next rack.
    - ○ this   ○ that   ● these

Subject and Object Pronouns

A **subject pronoun** takes the place of a noun or nouns as the subject of a sentence. Words, such as **I**, **you**, **she**, **he**, **it**, **we** and **they**, are subject pronouns.

Read each sentence. Underline the subject pronoun.

1. We are going to the dentist.

2. It won't take long.

3. I went in first.

4. She asked the assistant for help.

5. He gave the dentist some pink toothpaste.

6. They said the toothpaste would taste like strawberries.

7. You will like it too.

I
you
she
he
it
we
they

Decide which pronoun in the box can replace the underlined subject in the sentence. Write the pronoun on the line.

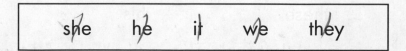

| she | he | it | we | they |

8. Dr Dell is a popular dentist. _____ he

9. Mrs Dell is his assistant. _____ she

10. The fox and the rabbit are waiting to be seen. _____ they

11. The fox has a bad toothache. _____ It

12. Roger and I enjoy reading the story. _____ we

© 2013 Scholastic Education International (S) Pte Ltd ISBN 978-981-07-5259-0

Subject and Object Pronouns

> An **object pronoun** takes the place of a noun or nouns as the object of a sentence. Words, such as **me**, **you**, **him**, **her**, **it**, **us** and **them**, are object pronouns.

Read each sentence. Underline the object pronoun.

1. Aunt Cindy gave <u>us</u> a football.

2. Our dog Rex found <u>it</u>.

3. He thinks the ball is for <u>him</u>.

4. I said, "Rex, that's not for <u>you</u>!"

5. Aunt Cindy gave <u>me</u> another ball for Rex.

6. Now, Rex always wants to play with <u>her</u>.

7. I like to watch <u>them</u>.

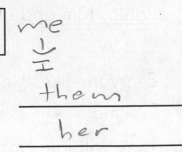

me
you
him
her
it
us
them

Decide which pronoun in the box can replace the underlined word or words in the sentence. Write the pronoun on the line.

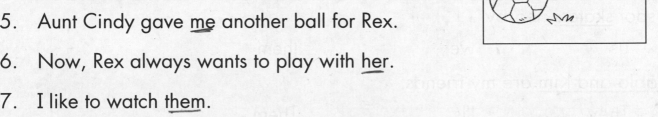

them	her	him	it	us

8. I went to the movies with <u>Rachel and Kevin</u>. _____ them

9. Kevin asked <u>Rachel</u> for some popcorn. _____ her

10. Rachel was happy to share <u>the popcorn</u>. _____ it

11. I accidentally bumped into <u>Kevin</u>. _____ him

12. The popcorn spilled all over <u>Rachel, Kevin and me</u>. _____ us

Date: _____

Subject and Object Pronouns

Decide which pronoun can replace the underlined word or words. Fill in the bubble next to the correct answer.

1. Uncle Sean is taking <u>Melina and me</u> ice skating at the pond.
   - ○ they
   - ● us
   - ○ her

2. <u>The pond</u> freezes by late December.
   - ○ He
   - ○ You
   - ● It

3. <u>Melina</u> knows how to skate.
   - ● She
   - ○ Her
   - ○ I

4. Uncle Sean shows <u>Melina</u> how to skate backward.
   - ● her
   - ○ she
   - ○ them

5. I spot <u>skaters</u> nearby.
   - ○ us
   - ○ we
   - ● them

6. <u>Pablo and Kim</u> are my friends.
   - ● They
   - ○ Us
   - ○ Them

7. <u>Uncle Sean</u> skates over to say hello.
   - ○ It
   - ● He
   - ○ Us

8. <u>Pablo, Kim and I</u> listen to Uncle Sean's jokes.
   - ● We
   - ○ Them
   - ○ Us

9. Everyone likes <u>Uncle Sean</u>.
   - ○ me
   - ○ he
   - ● him

10. They will join <u>Uncle Sean, Melina and me</u> for hot apple cider.
    - ● us
    - ○ we
    - ○ them

Possessive Forms

We use **possessive pronouns**, like *mine*, *yours*, *his*, *hers*, *ours* and *theirs*, to show ownership or belonging. We also use **possessive adjectives**, like *my*, *your*, *his*, *her*, *its*, *our* and *their*, to show ownership.

Read each pair of sentences. Underline the possessive adjective and circle the possessive pronoun.

1. These are my shoes. Those are yours.

2. The ballerina flats are hers. Those pink ones are also her shoes.

3. Jimmy can't find his sneakers. Are those his?

4. These kittens are ours. I think that one is their cat.

5. Can you give me your number? Here is mine.

6. This is our house. The house with the blue roof is theirs.

Complete each sentence with the correct possessive adjective from the box.

my	her	his	their	our

7. _____My_____ grandparents sent me a long letter in Spanish.

8. They said that ____their____ goal was to help me learn the language.

9. Grandmother included the words of __her__ favorite song.

10. Grandfather wrote a list of __his__ special tips for language learning.

11. During ____our____ next visit, we will try to speak more Spanish.

35

Date: _____

Possessive Forms

Circle the correct possessive form to complete each sentence.

1. My brother and I really enjoy visiting (our / ours) neighborhood library.

2. Every year, Ms Lee, the librarian, displays (hers / her) choices for the year's best reading.

3. Then, all the library users get to vote for (theirs / their) favorite books too.

4. The photo biography about Babe Ruth is (my / mine) favorite.

5. "Which is (yours / your)?" I asked my friends Penny and Dean.

6. They said that the *Lord of the Rings* series was (theirs / their).

Write sentences using the words provided.

7. his   favorite food   apple pie

   His favourite food is apple pie.

8. box of toy cars   theirs

   The box of toy cars must be theirs.

9. white milk bowl   our pet

   The white milk bowl is for our pet.

10. my friends love   their   favorite dish

   My friends love their favorite dish.

© 2013 Scholastic Education International (S) Pte Ltd ISBN 978-981-07-5259-0

Possessive Forms

Fill in the bubble next to the possessive adjective or pronoun that refers back to the underlined word or words and correctly completes each sentence.

1. I love baseball, and _____ hobby is collecting baseball cards.
   - ● my
   - ○ our
   - ○ your

2. Many <u>baseball card collectors</u> buy _____ cards from special dealers.
   - ○ your
   - ● their
   - ○ his

3. <u>Ralph</u> keeps _____ cards in an album.
   - ● his
   - ○ her
   - ○ my

4. This is where <u>I</u> keep _____.
   - ● mine
   - ○ yours
   - ○ my

5. This week, <u>Sue and I</u> will be going to _____ first baseball game.
   - ● our
   - ○ ours
   - ○ my

6. <u>These</u> tickets are _____.
   - ○ our
   - ● ours
   - ○ my

7. <u>The players</u> signed _____ names on my baseball cap.
   - ● their
   - ○ theirs
   - ○ your

8. <u>We</u> also bought _____ new baseball jerseys from the club house.
   - ● our
   - ○ ours
   - ○ my

9. <u>Jed</u> asked if these new jerseys are _____.
   - ● ours
   - ○ our
   - ○ her

10. <u>Sue</u> really treasures _____ new jersey.
    - ● her
    - ○ hers
    - ○ ours

Quantifiers

> A **quantifier** shows the amount or number of things. For countable nouns, we use quantifiers such as **few** and **many**. We can use **some**, **no**, **any**, and **a lot of** for both countable and uncountable nouns.

Underline the quantifier in each sentence.

1. Sally is making <u>some</u> cookies for the class party.

2. She only needs a <u>few</u> cups of flour to make these cookies.

3. She plans to add <u>many</u> raisins and nuts to the cookie dough.

4. She has to make sure <u>no</u> classmate is allergic to nuts.

5. There are <u>no</u> eggs in this recipe because Jen is allergic to eggs.

6. Does she want <u>any</u> icing sugar to decorate her cookies?

Circle the quantifier that best completes each sentence.

7. There are (some / **many**) vehicles on the road when the traffic is busy.

8. (**Some** / No) of them are large trucks and buses.

9. These heavy vehicles give out (many / **a lot of**) unhealthy fumes.

10. I usually don't see (none / **any**) bicycles on the road at this time.

11. (None / **No**) cyclist wants to be out there on the busy road.

12. There are (**many** / any) motorcycles moving between the lines of cars.

13. (**A few** / Any) of them have engines that make (many / a lot of) noise.

14. Luckily, there are (**none** / no) of those noisy motorcycles today.

38

Quantifiers

For uncountable nouns, we use quantifiers such as **much** and **a little**. We can use **some**, **no**, **none**, **any** and **a lot of** for countable and uncountable nouns.

Underline the quantifier in each sentence.

1. We made <u>many</u> sandwiches during our English class today.

2. First, we spread a <u>little</u> butter on two slices of bread.

3. Then, we placed a <u>few</u> pieces of lettuce on one slice of bread.

4. Next, we added <u>some</u> tuna onto the bread.

5. Finally, we sprinkled a <u>little</u> pepper on the tuna.

6. Darryl put too <u>much</u> pepper on his tuna.

7. He sneezed a <u>few</u> times.

8. Luckily, he did not get <u>any</u> lecture from Mrs Wu.

Circle the quantifier that best completes each sentence.

9. There are (many / much) people at the supermarket.

10. There is a special sale on (any / some) products sold here.

11. (Some / A little) items are sold at half the regular price.

12. Only (a little / a few) turkeys are left. They are almost sold out.

13. There is (much / no) applesauce at home.

14. Do we have (no / any) butter left?

15. Maybe we should get (a little / a few) bottles of soda.

Date: _____

Quantifiers

Fill in the bubble next to the quantifier that best completes each sentence.

1. We don't have _____ money left after our trip.
   - ○ many
   - ● much
   - ○ some

2. We spent _____ of money on the theme-park tickets.
   - ● a lot of
   - ○ any
   - ○ many

3. We visited _____ theme parks during our holiday.
   - ○ a little
   - ● a few
   - ○ none

4. _____ of the rides at the theme parks were too scary for me.
   - ● Some
   - ○ Much
   - ○ No

5. There was too _____ time to take all the rides at each park.
   - ○ few
   - ● little
   - ○ some

6. May I have _____ of your candy floss, please?
   - ○ a few
   - ● a little
   - ○ many

7. I won't take ___much___ of your candy floss.
   - ○ few
   - ○ little
   - ● much

8. I have _____ money left to buy my own.
   - ○ many
   - ● no
   - ○ none

9. I have _____ packets of raisins here with me.
   - ● a few
   - ○ a little
   - ○ any

10. Would you like _____ raisins to go with your candy floss?
    - ● any
    - ○ a little
    - ○ no

More Quantifiers

A **quantifier** can help compare amounts or number of things. For countable nouns, we use **more** or **fewer**. For uncountable nouns, we use **more** or **less**.

Complete each sentence with the correct quantifier – *more*, *less* or *fewer*.

1. John and Mimi are comparing to see who has __more__ books.

2. John has __fewer__ storybooks than Mimi because he does not read stories.

3. However, he has __more__ non-fiction books than Mimi.

4. He likes books with __fewer__ pictures and more text.

5. Mimi, on the other hand, prefers books with more pictures but __less__ text.

6. Although John has __fewer__ books than Mimi, his books are thicker.

7. Mimi may have more books than John, but her books have __less__ pages.

8. John thinks that the more he reads, the __more__ knowledge he will gain.

9. He spends __less__ time on sports than many boys his age.

10. Mimi is buying __fewer__ books these days as she has too many.

11. She has __less__ empty space in her room than her brother because her books take up so much space.

12. She will go to the library if she wants to read __more__ books.

More Quantifiers

> A **quantifier** shows the amount or number of things. Some, like **each** and **both**, tell the exact number while others, such as **enough** and **plenty of**, do not.

Underline the quantifier in each sentence.

1. There are <u>many</u> rules in Duxton Elementary School.

2. <u>All</u> students have to wear a tie to school.

3. <u>No</u> stall in the canteen is allowed to sell drinks.

4. There are <u>plenty of</u> watercoolers throughout the school.

5. <u>Each</u> student has to bring his own tumbler to school daily.

6. The teachers will check that students drink <u>enough</u> water <u>each</u> day.

7. Frank and Joe have to fill their tumblers <u>several</u> times a day.

Complete each sentence using a suitable quantifier from the sentences above.

8. As a rule, __all__ students have to report to the hall every morning.

9. __Noch__ student is allowed to go to the classroom first.

10. In the hall, __each__ teacher will take the students' attendance.

11. Frank and Joe have been late __many__ times this year.

12. Tomorrow, they will get up early so that they have __penoughhf__ time to get ready for school.

More Quantifiers

Read each sentence. Fill in the bubble next to the quantifier.

1. I have less time than I thought.
   ○ I   ● less   ○ than

2. There are more questions in this assignment than yesterday's.
   ● more   ○ assignment   ○ yesterday's

3. I need plenty of help from my brother.
   ○ need   ● plenty of   ○ from

4. Every solution has to be shown in full.
   ○ Every   ○ solution   ● full

5. I won't have enough rest tonight.
   ○ won't   ● enough   ○ tonight

Fill in the bubble next to the quantifier that best completes each sentence.

6. There were _____ people at the restaurant today.
   ● more   ○ less   ○ plenty

7. Almost _____ table was occupied.
   ○ all   ● every   ○ many

8. We got a table after waiting _____ minutes.
   ● a few   ○ a little   ○ more

9. _____ of us were very hungry.
   ● All   ○ Every   ○ Plenty

10. We wanted to order _____ of food.
   ○ all   ● plenty   ○ enough

Action Verbs

> An **action verb** shows action. Some action verbs name actions that can be seen. Others, such as **think**, name actions that can't be seen.

Underline the action verb in each sentence.

1. Judy Hindley <u>wrote</u> a book about the history of string.

2. An illustrator <u>painted</u> funny pictures about string.

3. Long ago, people <u>twisted</u> vines into long ropes.

4. People still <u>weave</u> long, thin fibers into cloth.

5. My sister <u>knits</u> sweaters from thick wool yarn.

6. We <u>stretched</u> the rope hammock from tree to tree.

7. I always <u>tie</u> a ribbon around a birthday package.

8. We <u>learned</u> about different kinds of knots.

9. He <u>made</u> a belt from three different colors of string.

10. We <u>wished</u> for another book by Judy Hindley.

Action Verbs

Read each sentence. Underline the action verb that is more vivid.

1. The rabbit quickly (moved / (hopped)) across the lawn.

2. We (sat / (lounged)) on the chairs near the pool.

3. I ((pounded) / touched) the nail with my hammer.

4. The thirsty dog (drank / (slurped)) the water noisily.

5. I (made / (sewed)) a quilt from the scraps of fabric.

6. The horses (go / (galloped)) across the field.

7. Minna and Max ((gulped) / ate) their sandwiches in a hurry.

8. The workers ((dragged) / moved) the heavy load across the yard.

Write sentences using the action verbs in brackets.

9. (follow) __I followed him_____

10. (shout) __I shouted at my son._____

11. (rush) __I rushed to work_____

12. (slip) __I had slipped on the water while Jet-
skiing__

Date: _____

Action Verbs

Read each sentence. Fill in the bubble next to the action verb.

1. The space shuttle circled Earth twenty times.
    ○ space   ● circled   ○ twenty

2. Yesterday morning, my class watched the newscast on TV.
    ○ morning   ○ class   ● watched

3. I think about space exploration all the time.
    ● think   ○ exploration   ○ time

4. Before a mission, astronauts train for months.
    ○ mission   ● train   ○ months

5. She read a biography about the first woman in space.
    ● read   ○ about   ○ space

Fill in the bubble next to the more vivid action verb.

6. At the beach, we _____ for pieces of driftwood.
    ○ looked   ● hunted

7. We _____ into the foamy waves.
    ○ walked   ● plunged

8. Several artists _____ a huge castle out of sand.
    ● sculpted   ○ made

9. I _____ my beach towel under a large umbrella.
    ○ put   ● spread

10. A wild horses _____ along the sandy seashore.
    ● galloped   ○ ran

Date: _____

Subject-Verb Agreement

> The subject and verb of a sentence must agree in number – both must be singular or both must be plural. If the subject of a sentence is singular, we often add **–s** or **–es** to the verb. If the subject is plural, we do not add **–s**.

Read each sentence. Underline the subject and circle the verb.

1. Tucker lives in a drainpipe.

2. It opens into a pocket.

3. Tucker collected stuffing for the pocket.

4. The mouse filled the pocket with paper and cloth.

5. Tucker sits at the opening of the drainpipe.

6. He watches the people in the subway station.

Read each sentence. Underline the subject and circle the verb. Then, write *singular* if the subject and verb are singular and *plural* if the subject and verb are plural.

7. The crowd passes by quickly. _____ S _____

8. Trains run less often at that time. _____ P _____

9. Papa waits for business. _____ S _____

10. The station feels quiet and lonely. _____ S _____

11. People rush home at the end of the day. _____ P _____

12. Mama and Papa make very little money. _____ P _____

Subject-Verb Agreement

Circle the correct form of the verb in brackets to complete each sentence.

1. Crickets ((make) / makes) a musical sound.

2. Actually, only the males ((produce) / produces) sounds.

3. I ((listen) / listens) for the sound of crickets on a summer night.

4. You ((hear) / hears) them in places outside the city.

5. Mario ((finds) / find) a cricket in the subway station.

6. His mother ((calls) / call) the cricket a bug.

Underline the subject and verb in each sentence. Then, rewrite each sentence in the present tense. Be sure the subject and verb agree.

7. Mario wanted the cricket for a pet.

   Mario wants the cricket for a pet.

8. He wished for a pet of his own.

   He wishes for a pet of his own.

9. Crickets seemed like unusual pets to his mother.

   Crickets seems like unusual pets to himmom

10. Maybe insects scared her!

    Maybe insects scares her!!!

© 2013 Scholastic Education International (S) Pte Ltd ISBN 978-981-07-5259-0

Assessment

Date: _____

Subject-Verb Agreement

Circle the verb that agrees with the subject.

Chester 1.(see / sees) tall buildings for the first time.

The city 2. (surprise / surprises) him. The stars

3. (catch / catches) Chester's attention. Maybe he

4. (long / longs) for his old home. One star

5. (seem / seems) familiar to Chester.

Is the underlined verb in each sentence correct? Fill in the bubble next to the correct answer.

6. Now the animals <u>crouch</u> against the cement.

   ○ crouches   ○ crouched   ● correct as is

7. At this moment, their eyes <u>is</u> on the sky.

   ● are   ○ were   ○ correct as is

8. The sky <u>looks</u> so beautiful right now!

   ○ look   ○ looked   ● correct as is

9. Last night, the mouse <u>view</u> Times Square for the first time.

   ● views   ○ viewed   ○ correct as is

10. A week ago, Chester <u>experiences</u> a far different world.

   ○ experience   ● experienced   ○ correct as is

Articles

The words **a**, **an** and **the** are **articles.** We use **a** before words that begin with a consonant. We use **an** before words that begin with a vowel. We use **the** when we are referring to something specific.

Underline the article(s) in each sentence.

1. We reached the airport an hour before the plane took off.

2. I carried a small suitcase as well as an old shoulder bag.

3. Sis had two bags too, and a pair of headphones around her neck.

4. We were going on a family vacation to Hong Kong.

5. We had to make our way through the crowded airport.

6. An air stewardess greeted us as we boarded the plane.

7. She did not look pleased as we were the last to board.

8. My seat was next to the window, beside a child about my age.

9. We chatted with each other all the way to Hong Kong.

Complete the sentences with the articles *a*, *an* or *the*.

10. We took __a__ train from the airport to the city.

11. Then, we caught __a__ cab to get to our hotel.

12. At __the__ hotel, we had to wait for our rooms to be ready.

13. While waiting, we could have __a__ free meal at the lounge.

14. I ordered __an__ éclair and __a__ cup of hot chocolate.

15. Sis ate __the__ entire pizza all by herself.

Articles

> An **article** is a word that usually comes before a noun. Sometimes, we do not need to use an article before the noun.

Cross out the unnecessary article in each sentence.

1. Pandas are ~~the~~ rare members of the bear family.
2. They live in bamboo forests in ~~a~~ western China.
3. Pandas eat ~~the~~ nothing but bamboo.
4. They have a black and ~~a~~ white fur coat.
5. They are ~~the~~ excellent tree climbers.
6. ~~The~~ children all over the world adore the panda.
7. A newborn panda is the size of a stick of ~~a~~ butter.
8. It can grow up to ~~the~~ 330 pounds as an adult.
9. In ~~the~~ China, the panda is a national treasure.
10. These cuddly bears are on the edge of ~~an~~ extinction.

Complete the sentences with the articles *a*, *an* or *the*. Leave a blank if the article is not needed.

11. A group of about _____ 30 people visited __the__ Singapore zoo early one morning
12. They were there to see __the__ pandas Kai Kai and Jia Jia.
13. __A__ long queue started forming at 8 in __the__ morning.
14. __The__ early birds wanted to beat __the__ crowd.
15. One of these was Ken, who said he was __an__ animal lover.
16. You can see the pandas at __The__ Giant Panda Forest, __a a__ new tourist attraction.

Date: _____

Articles   *a an the*

Fill in the bubble next to the article that correctly completes each sentence.

1. There are many local festivals in _____ Japan.
   ○ a   ○ the   ● no article

2. They are usually celebrated once _____ year.
   ● a   ○ an   ○ the

3. Some of _____ festivals last over many days.
   ○ a   ● the   ○ no article

4. In February, you can see large snow sculptures in _____ city park in Sapporo.
   ● a   ○ the   ○ no article

5. In spring and _____ autumn, large pretty floats are pulled through Takayama town.
   ○ a   ○ the   ● no article

6. _____ important festival is the Tenjin Matsuri, when there are fireworks.
   ○ A   ● An   ○ The

7. _____ interesting dancing festival is held in mid-August in Tokushima City.
   ○ A   ● An   ● The

8. In October, in Kyoto, _____ huge historical parade begins from the palace.
   ● a   ● the   ○ no article

9. On 3 December, _____ city of Chichibu celebrates the Night Festival with fireworks and music.
   ○ a   ● the   ○ no article

10. Most of _____ festivals have a religious background.
    ○ a   ● the   ○ no article

Modals

A **modal** is a helping verb that can express ability, permission or obligation. Sometimes, the negative **not** comes after a modal verb.

Underline the modal verb in each sentence.

1. Tourists may enter the hot springs museum.

2. All visitors must remove their shoes before they enter.

3. They can change into the slippers provided.

4. Visitors may visit all the rooms except the office.

5. They must not enter the office at all times.

6. You can stay as long as you like while the museum is open.

7. Visitors should keep their voices down in the museum.

Circle the better modal verb to complete each sentence.

8. You (can / should) make a terrarium in less than an hour.

9. Ask your mother if you (may / should) use a nice empty bottle of hers.

10. Any glass container with a wide mouth (can / must) be used.

11. The plants (can / should) not touch the sides, so choose a wide jar.

Modals

A **modal** can also express different extents of possibility. For example, **will** is more certain than **may**, which is in turn more likely than **might**.

Which sentence shows the greatest certainty? Write (1) for "most certain", (2) for "fairly certain" and (3) for "least certain".

1. (a) The weather girl reported that it will rain today.   *1*
   (b) Grandmother thinks that it may rain today.   *2*
   (c) It looks like it might rain, so bring an umbrella.   *3*

2. (a) I might go to the party, but I haven't decided yet.   *3*
   (b) Amy may not go to the party if it rains.   *2*
   (c) Sam will be going to the party whether or not it rains.   *1*

3. (a) You might see a clown at the party.   *3*
   (b) There will be lots of food and balloons.   *1*
   (c) Taylor may sing a song at the party.   *2*

Write sentences about the party using the given modal and verb.

4. will not stay

   The troll hunter will not stay in Troll market for long.

5. may cut

   The eclipse sword may cut Gunmar's head.

6. might play

   Toby might play the Gronka mask while dim is in the darklands.

54

Date: _____

Modals

Fill in the bubble next to the modal that best completes the sentence.

1. You _____ go on all the rides.
    ○ may not   ○ cannot   ● should not

2. You _____ be taller than 1 meter to take some of the rides.
    ○ may   ○ can   ● must

3. You _____ also be fit and not have motion sickness.
    ○ may   ○ can   ● must

4. Otherwise, you _____ feel really sick after the ride.
    ● may   ○ should   ○ must

5. With this ticket, you _____ take as many rides as you like.
    ● will   ○ can   ○ must

6. You _____ be patient and wait for your turn in the queue.
    ● should   ○ may   ○ can

7. Remember that you _____ keep your hands on the bar during the ride.
    ○ may   ○ can   ● must

8. Accidents _____ occur if people do not obey the safety rules.
    ● may   ○ should   ○ must

9. Dad said he _____ take us there again next month if the prices come down.
    ● might   ○ can   ○ must

10. We _____ let you know if we are going, so we can visit the park together.
    ○ can   ● will   ○ should

More Modals

A modal is a helping verb that comes before a main verb to express a special meaning. We can use **modals** to make an offer, a request or a suggestion. The main verb that follows should be in the base form.

Underline the modal and circle the main verb it goes with.

1. Would you like me to take your coat?

2. May I get you a hot drink?

3. I could switch off the fan, if you like.

4. What else can I do for you?

5. Could you show me the way to the hotel, please?

6. May I have a copy of the city map?

7. Can you help me with my bags, please?

8. Shall we go out for dinner tonight?

9. We could try the food at the new pizza place.

Write an offer, request or suggestion starting with the given modal.

10. Would _____

11. Could _____

12. Shall _____

© 2013 Scholastic Education International (S) Pte Ltd ISBN 978-981-07-5259-0

More Modals

> Less common **modals** are **ought to**, **have to** and **need to**. They come before main verbs to express obligation, compulsion or necessity, and are sometimes called **semi-modals**. To form the negative, we simply add **not** after **need** or **ought**.

Circle the modal, in brackets, which is closer in meaning to the underlined words.

1. Yano <u>should</u> visit his sick grandmother (has to / ought to).

2. He <u>must</u> get there before 9 p.m. (has to / ought to). The last bus leaves at 9.30.

3. He <u>should</u> show more concern for his grandparents (has to / ought to).

4. He <u>is required to</u> show his ID at the hospital counter (ought to / needs to).

5. He <u>should</u> offer her some flowers when he sees her (has to / ought to).

6. The flowers <u>must</u> be wrapped or else they will not let him bring them in (have to / ought to).

Change each sentence to the negative by adding *not* to the modal.

7. You ought to spend time on your Math.

    _____

8. James needs to ask Ms Peters for help.

    _____

9. She ought to give him extra lessons in Math.

    _____

© 2013 Scholastic Education International (S) Pte Ltd ISBN 978-981-07-5259-0

More Modals

Fill in the bubble next to the modal that best completes the sentence.

1. You _____ take a rest after that long walk.
   - ○ need
   - ○ ought to
   - ○ might

2. _____ I help you with that heavy bag?
   - ○ Ought
   - ○ Have
   - ○ May

3. _____ you like me to get you an iced tea?
   - ○ May
   - ○ Would
   - ○ Can

4. You _____ lean back in that comfortable chair.
   - ○ could
   - ○ would
   - ○ need

5. _____ we turn on some music to help you relax?
   - ○ Would
   - ○ Shall
   - ○ May

6. _____ you kindly remove your shoes before stepping in here?
   - ○ Need
   - ○ Could
   - ○ May

7. Visitors _____ read the rules written on the board.
   - ○ ought to
   - ○ shall
   - ○ would

8. They _____ remove their socks unless they want to.
   - ○ shall
   - ○ must
   - ○ need not

9. _____ you follow me now to the showroom?
   - ○ Ought
   - ○ Would
   - ○ May

10. We _____ spend an hour here if you like.
    - ○ need
    - ○ must
    - ○ could

© 2013 Scholastic Education International (S) Pte Ltd ISBN 978-981-07-5259-0

Reflexive Pronouns

> A **reflexive pronoun** refers to the person or thing that is the subject of the sentence. It ends with **-self** for singular pronouns, and **-selves** for plural pronouns.

Underline the reflexive pronoun in each sentence, and circle the subject that it refers to.

1. Ellen hurt herself during the soccer match yesterday.

2. The referee blamed himself for her injury.

3. Ellen wanted to score the goal herself.

4. The opponent team played well and were proud of themselves.

5. They gave themselves a treat at the new burger restaurant.

6. We were enjoying ourselves at the game until Ellen fell.

7. After the game, Ellen limped home herself.

Complete each sentence with a suitable reflexive pronoun.

8. "Behave _____ at the party," Mom reminded us.

9. We found our way to Betty's house _____.

10. Betty baked the birthday cake _____.

11. Her brothers introduced _____ as Tom and Jerry.

12. Tom made a fool of _____ during the games.

13. I nearly cut _____ with the knife.

Reflexive Pronouns

Reflexive pronouns are sometimes used to emphasize the subject.

Underline the reflexive pronoun in each sentence, and circle the subject that it emphasizes.

1. The principal himself will attend the concert.

2. We ourselves will welcome him at the door.

3. The girls themselves put up the decorations.

4. My sister herself sewed her own costume.

5. I myself will prepare the drinks.

6. You yourself are responsible for the food.

7. The concert itself will take 90 minutes. The reception comes after that.

Complete each sentence using the given subject and a suitable reflexive pronoun.

8. The little boy _____.

9. His mother _____.

10. Their pet dog _____.

11. Grandpa _____.

12. The neighbors _____.

Reflexive Pronouns

Read each sentence. Fill in the bubble next to the subject that the reflexive pronoun refers to.

1. You are too young to go to the movies yourself.
   ○ You   ○ young   ○ movies

2. Dad is driving himself to his office.
   ○ office   ○ himself   ○ Dad

3. Grandpa himself will accompany you to the movies.
   ○ Grandpa   ○ himself   ○ you

4. Our cat Whiskers can look after itself at home.
   ○ Our   ○ Whiskers   ○ home

5. Mom is going to treat herself to a visit at the spa.
   ○ visit   ○ Mom   ○ spa

Fill in the bubble next to the reflexive pronoun that correctly completes the sentence.

6. Did you write this story _____?
   ○ yours   ○ yourself   ○ myself

7. How does the man in the story make _____ invisible?
   ○ herself   ○ yourself   ○ himself

8. What is the dog doing to _____ in this story?
   ○ myself   ○ itself   ○ themselves

9. Why can't the girls save _____?
   ○ herself   ○ himself   ○ themselves

10. I wish I could be so creative _____.
    ○ yourself   ○ myself   ○ ourselves

Adjectives

Adjectives describe nouns. They can tell what color, size and shape something is. They can also tell how something sounds, feels or tastes.

Read the sentences. Underline the adjectives that tell what kind and circle the adjectives that tell how many.

1. We watched many colorful creatures swim through the dark water.

2. A few tilefish were building small burrows.

3. Suddenly, one strange and unusual fish swam by us.

4. Eugene swam over to the mysterious fish.

5. It looked like a jawfish with a big head and four dark patches on its back.

6. Was this rare fish a new species?

7. We put the tiny fish in a large bucket of cold seawater.

8. Eugene has made several amazing discoveries.

Write two sentences. Use adjectives that tell what kind and how many in each sentence.

9. _____

10. _____

Adjectives

Complete each sentence with a suitable adjective.

1. The _____ dog ate most of the cat's food.

2. The _____ cat found a nearly empty bowl.

3. The cat ate what remained of her _____ meal.

4. The cat pushed the _____ dish over to where a
    _____ girl was sitting.

5. The girl refilled the dish with _____ food.

Read each sentence. Circle the adjective that describes each underlined noun.

6. The gray <u>cat</u> saw the shaggy <u>dog</u> sitting in the dark <u>corner</u>.

7. The cat saw some <u>cat food</u> on the dog's droopy <u>mouth</u>.

8. The cat slipped out of the little <u>kitchen</u> and went into the quiet <u>backyard</u>.

9. She started digging in the soft <u>dirt</u> under a shady <u>tree</u>.

10. The dog looked out the enormous <u>window</u> and saw the cat with a
    large <u>bone</u>.

Write two sentences that tell what happened next. Use vivid adjectives in
your writing.

11. _____

12. _____

Date: _____

Adjectives

Complete each sentence with an adjective that tells what kind or how many.

1. The _____ fish was named after David.

2. The fish had a _____ head.

3. The fish lived in a _____ burrow at the bottom of the ocean.

4. The tiny fish turned out to be a _____ species.

5. David took _____ photographs that appeared in magazines.

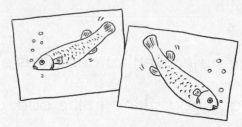

Read each sentence. Fill in the bubble next to the word that is an adjective.

6. I had an important decision to make this morning.
   ○ important   ○ decision   ○ morning

7. I wanted to buy a suitable gift for my sister.
   ○ wanted   ○ suitable   ○ sister

8. I considered getting two hamsters.
   ○ considered   ○ getting   ○ two

9. I also thought of getting a noisy parrot.
   ○ thought   ○ noisy   ○ parrot

10. Finally, I decided to get a saltwater aquarium.
   ○ decided   ○ saltwater   ○ aquarium

Order of Adjectives

Sometimes, two or more **adjectives** come before a noun to tell more about it. We need to arrange them in a certain order: quality – size – age – shape – color – type.

For each sentence, underline the adjectives that tell more about a noun. Circle the noun.

1. Sal has a large, blue plastic suitcase.

2. She bought it from a little old luggage shop in Chinatown.

3. The suitcase contains many small, white cardboard boxes.

4. Each box is filled with expensive, colorful postage stamps from all over the world.

5. She got her stamps from her kind, elderly maternal uncle.

6. She is now looking for an elegant, large collector's album to display her stamps.

Fill in the bubble next to the sentence that has the adjectives in the right order.

7. ○ I saw many types of beautiful, colorful tropical fish.
   ○ I saw many types of tropical, beautiful colorful fish.
   ○ I saw many types of colorful, tropical beautiful fish.

8. ○ Some tanks were rectangular, large, boring glass containers.
   ○ Some tanks were boring, large, rectangular glass containers.
   ○ Some tanks were boring, glass, rectangular large containers.

9. ○ Others were modern, round fiberglass tanks.
   ○ Others were round, modern fiberglass tanks.
   ○ Others were modern, fiberglass round tanks.

Order of Adjectives

Complete each sentence with a suitable adjective that tells more about the noun.

1. New York is a _____, cosmopolitan American city.

2. In the city are several tall, _____, square office buildings.

3. The Met is a popular modern _____ museum containing many paintings and sculptures.

4. In the middle of the city lies Central Park, a large, _____ leisure space with many trees and plants.

Write a sentence containing the given noun and adjectives in the right order.

5. noun: flowers   adjectives: plastic, old, ugly

    _____

6. noun: dress   adjectives: pink, pretty, silk, long

    _____

7. noun: boy   adjectives: skinny, Italian, young

    _____

8. noun: market   adjectives: crowded, huge, square

    _____

Order of Adjectives

Fill in the bubble next to the right order of adjectives that completes each sentence.

1. Grandma saw some _____ tomatoes on display at the vegetable stall.

   ○ juicy, large, round cherry
   ○ large, cherry, round juicy
   ○ round, juicy, cherry large

2. She took out some money from her _____ purse.

   ○ worn-out, plastic brown
   ○ worn-out, brown plastic
   ○ brown, plastic worn-out

3. The seller was a cheerful man with _____ teeth.

   ○ crooked, front yellow
   ○ yellow, front crooked
   ○ crooked, yellow front

4. He pointed at the _____ beans at the next table.

   ○ green, French fresh
   ○ fresh, green French
   ○ French, green, fresh

5. Both the tomatoes and beans went into Grandma's _____ shopping basket.

   ○ large, ancient bamboo
   ○ ancient, bamboo large
   ○ bamboo, large ancient

6. My family went shopping at the _____ store in town yesterday.

   ○ modern, budget huge
   ○ huge, modern budget
   ○ budget, huge modern

Adjectives That Compare

Comparative adjectives compare two things by adding **–er** to the adjective or by using the word **more**. **Superlative adjectives** compare three or more things by adding **–est** or by using the word **most**.

Underline the adjective that compares in each sentence.

1. Anna is older than her brother Caleb.

2. That was the loudest thunderstorm of the entire summer.

3. The roof of the barn is higher than the top of the haystack.

4. The kitten's fur was softer than lamb's wool.

5. Sarah pointed to the brightest star in the sky.

6. What is the saddest moment in the story?

Circle the adjective in brackets that completes each sentence correctly. Write *two* or *more than two* to show how many things are being compared.

7. We went swimming on the (hottest / hotter) day in July. _____

8. Today is (warmer / warmest) than last Friday. _____

9. This is the (taller / tallest) tree in the park. _____

10. Sarah's hair is (longer / longest) than Maggie's. _____

11. Nikky was the (friendlier / friendliest) dog in the pound. _____

12. Caleb's horse is (younger / youngest) than Anna's. _____

© 2013 Scholastic Education International (S) Pte Ltd ISBN 978-981-07-5259-0

Adjectives That Compare

Complete each sentence with the correct adjective from the box.

| funnier | funniest |

1. The _____ book I've ever read is about a family of mice.

2. The book is much _____ than the movie.

| busier | busiest |

3. The book department is _____ than the shoe department.

4. The _____ bookstore in the city is on King Street.

| more exciting | most exciting |

5. Hiking in the woods is _____ than watching TV.

6. This is the _____ ride at the amusement park.

| more challenging | most challenging |

7. Is the game of checkers _____ than the game of chess?

8. I think that soccer is the _____ of all the field games.

| more tiring | most tiring |

9. We found that swimming was _____ than walking.

10. Of all the activities, tennis was the _____.

| more delicious | most delicious |

11. The strawberries are _____ than the grapes.

12. This is the _____ apple that I have ever eaten.

Assessment

Date: _____

Adjectives That Compare

Fill in the bubble next to the correct comparative or superlative adjective.

1. I believe that a dog is much _____ than a cat.
   ○ friendlier   ○ friendliest

2. The poodle is the _____ dog of all the dogs in the pound.
   ○ more intelligent   ○ most intelligent

3. The gazelle is the _____ animal in the animal park.
   ○ more graceful   ○ most graceful

4. The movie about turtles is _____ than the book about frogs.
   ○ more fascinating   ○ most fascinating

5. A rattlesnake is _____ than a bull snake.
   ○ more dangerous   ○ most dangerous

6. I think that the jaguar is the _____ of all the big cats.
   ○ more beautiful   ○ most beautiful

7. Did you know that a cheetah is _____ than a lion?
   ○ swifter   ○ swiftest

8. Your parrot is _____ than my cockatoo.
   ○ noisier   ○ noisiest

9. This chimpanzee is _____ than that gorilla.
   ○ more playful   ○ most playful

10. That polar bear is the _____ mammal I've ever seen.
    ○ larger   ○ largest

© 2013 Scholastic Education International (S) Pte Ltd ISBN 978-981-07-5259-0

Adjectives Ending in *-ed* or *-ing*

> **Adjectives ending in *-ed* or *-ing*** can be confusing. An *-ed* adjective (e.g. **bored**) usually tells how a person feels; an *-ing* adjective (e.g. **boring**) usually describes the thing or person that causes the feeling.

Read each sentence. Does the underlined adjective tell more about a person or thing? Circle the noun and underline *person* or *thing*.

1. It was an <u>exciting</u> day for the family. (person / thing)

2. Dad and Mom were <u>thrilled</u> that Jose was in the finals for the race. (person / thing)

3. His start was <u>encouraging</u>, and they expected him to do very well. (person/ thing)

4. After running for ten minutes, Jose looked <u>tired</u> and slowed down. (person / thing)

5. His parents found his slow pace <u>alarming</u>. (person / thing)

6. His coach was <u>alarmed</u> by the drop in speed. (person / thing)

7. But Jose shocked everyone by sprinting at an <u>amazing</u> speed near the end. (person / thing)

8. We were <u>pleased</u> to see him come in first. (person / thing)

Write sentences using the adjectives in brackets.

9. (excited) _____

10. (exciting) _____

11. (surprised) _____

12. (surprising) _____

Adjectives Ending in *-ed* or *-ing*

Circle the correct adjective to complete each sentence.

1. The show on television was really (boring / bored).

2. Joan was so (boring / bored) that she fell asleep on the sofa.

3. But when she got to her bed, she was (annoying / annoyed) that she did not feel sleepy anymore.

4. So, she started to read the book that Dad said had an (interesting / interested) plot.

5. Indeed, she was not (disappointing / disappointed).

6. The story turned out to be really (fascinating / fascinated).

7. When her parents got home, they were (surprised / surprising) to see her up so late.

Add *-ed* or *-ing* to each word in brackets to complete each sentence. Write the adjective on the line.

8. My sister was _____ (embarrass) when she fell from her wheelchair today.

9. Her classmate found it _____ (amuse) and laughed at her.

10. I was _____ (disgust) by the unkind classmate.

11. I also felt _____ (concern) for my sister.

12. She needs to be surrounded by _____ (encourage) friends.

© 2013 Scholastic Education International (S) Pte Ltd ISBN 978-981-07-5259-0

Adjectives Ending in *-ed* or *-ing*

Read each sentence. What word does the underlined adjective describe?
Fill in the bubble next to the word.

1. Faizal is <u>frustrated</u> with the difficult homework from school.
   ○ Faizal   ○ homework   ○ school

2. He feels that many of the questions were <u>confusing</u>.
   ○ He   ○ questions   ○ feels

3. Faizal has been <u>interested</u> in Mathematics since he was a child.
   ○ Faizal   ○ Mathematics   ○ child

4. He used to get <u>excited</u> whenever he solved a difficult problem.
   ○ He   ○ solved   ○ problem

5. Now, he finds the subject <u>depressing</u> as he cannot solve the problems.
   ○ subject   ○ he   ○ problems

Fill in the bubble next to the adjective that best completes each sentence.

6. We watched an _____ game show on television yesterday.
   ○ entertained   ○ entertaining

7. The activities on the show were quite _____.
   ○ amused   ○ amusing

8. The participants had to complete various _____ tasks.
   ○ challenged   ○ challenging

9. The support from the live audience was most _____.
   ○ encouraged   ○ encouraging

10. I was _____ by how sporting and cheerful the participants were.
    ○ amazed   ○ amazing

Irregular Verbs

An **irregular verb** does not form the past tense by adding **-ed**. It is spelt differently in the past tense.

Underline the irregular verb in each sentence.

1. This morning, Mom bought a red and a green toothbrush.

2. Pat made a tuna sandwich in the kitchen.

3. Mom quickly came into the dining room.

4. Deever rode her bicycle over to Pat's house.

5. Deever shook her head in great amusement.

6. They heard a great deal of noise in the kitchen.

7. Deever took a close look at the toothbrushes.

Circle the irregular past tense verb in brackets. Then, write it on the line to complete the sentence.

8. We _____ a funny story about toothbrushes. (hear / heard)

9. Pat _____ his decision after a few minutes. (made / make)

10. Mom _____ him an orange toothbrush. (bought / buy)

11. Pat _____ into a smile. (broke / break)

12. We _____ he would never make up his mind. (think / thought)

Irregular Verbs

> An **irregular verb** does not form the past tense by adding **–ed**. The past participle is the form of the verb used with **has**, **have**, **had** or **will have**.

Underline the helping verb and the irregular past participle in each sentence.

1. We have chosen a fantastic day for our school picnic.

2. Mr Torr has brought all the food and beverages in his van.

3. We have eaten all of the carrots on the table.

4. Ms Chang has hidden the prizes for the treasure hunt.

5. By noon our teacher had taken over forty photographs.

6. All the students have gone on a short walk to the lake.

7. They had heard about the paddleboats there.

8. Some of my friends have ridden in the boats.

Complete each sentence by circling the correct past participle in brackets.

9. By May I had (hear / heard) about an amazing automobile.

10. Test drivers have (taken / took) it on experimental runs.

11. My friend's family has (gone / went) to Utah to see it.

12. My friend has (ridden / rode) in the automobile, too.

13. I have (chosen / chose) this car as a research topic.

14. I have (bring / brought) articles and books about the car.

Irregular Verbs

Fill in the bubble next to the correct irregular verb.

1. Last week, we _____ the news about our baseball team's victory.
   - ○ hear
   - ○ heard
   - ○ hears

2. Yesterday, Mom and I _____ the bus downtown.
   - ○ rode
   - ○ rides
   - ○ ride

3. Then, we _____ in line for an hour.
   - ○ stand
   - ○ stood
   - ○ stands

4. We finally _____ four tickets to the first game.
   - ○ bought
   - ○ buys
   - ○ buying

5. Then, we _____ lunch to celebrate.
   - ○ eat
   - ○ ate
   - ○ eats

Fill in the bubble next to the correct helping verb and past participle.

6. That old house _____ on top of the hill for a century.
   - ○ has stood
   - ○ has stand
   - ○ has stands

7. We _____ up there many times.
   - ○ have rode
   - ○ have ride
   - ○ have ridden

8. Our great-grandfather _____ pictures of the house long ago.
   - ○ had drawn
   - ○ had draw
   - ○ had drew

9. We _____ the sketches for many years.
   - ○ have kept
   - ○ have keep
   - ○ have keeps

10. My family _____ very good care of the drawings.
    - ○ has took
    - ○ has take
    - ○ has taken

Verb Tenses

Present tense verbs show action that is happening now or on a regular basis. **Past tense verbs** show action that took place in the past. **Future tense verbs** show action that will happen in the future.

Write *present* if the underlined word is a present tense verb, *past* if it is a past tense verb, and *future* if it is a future tense verb on the line.

1. The story of sneakers <u>started</u> with the development of rubber. _____

2. People in Central and South America <u>melted</u> gum from trees. _____

3. We <u>will visit</u> two museums. _____

4. Everyone <u>will carry</u> a small backpack. _____

5. Rubber <u>protected</u> the wearer's feet. _____

6. However, pure rubber <u>cracks</u> in cold weather. _____

7. Charles Goodyear <u>believed</u> in a solution. _____

8. The shoe companies <u>manufactured</u> shoes with rubber soles. _____

Choose four past tense verbs from the sentences above and form sentences with their present tense forms.

9. _____

10. _____

11. _____

12. _____

Verb Tenses

Complete each sentence with the correct form of the verb in brackets.

1. Anna _____ (wear) dark purple sneakers to school today.

2. She _____ (step) onto something dirty yesterday.

3. Her white sneakers _____ (be) in the wash today.

4. Her purple sneakers _____ (hurt) her feet as they are a bit too small.

5. She _____ (buy) new ones if her feet hurt too much.

6. She _____ (want) comfortable sneakers.

Write sentences using the present, past and future tense form of the verb as indicated in brackets.

7. (walk – *past tense*) _____

8. (cry – *future tense*) _____

9. (jump – *present tense*) _____

10. (buy – *past tense*) _____

11. (fall – *future tense*) _____

12. (eat – *present tense*) _____

© 2013 Scholastic Education International (S) Pte Ltd ISBN 978-981-07-5259-0

Assessment

Verb Tenses

Look at the underlined verb or verbs. Fill in the bubble next to the correct tense.

1. Tomorrow we <u>will march</u> in the National Day parade.
   ○ past   ○ present   ○ future

2. Last week, my sister and I <u>sewed</u> our own costumes.
   ○ past   ○ present   ○ future

3. Many other people <u>will dress</u> as our country's pioneers.
   ○ past   ○ present   ○ future

4. Everyone <u>participates</u> in the celebration.
   ○ past   ○ present   ○ future

5. <u>Will</u> the people <u>cheer</u> us on?
   ○ past   ○ present   ○ future

Decide if the underlined verbs are correct. Fill in the bubble next to the correct answer.

6. The parade <u>will began</u> in the late afternoon.
   ○ will begin   ○ will begins   ○ correct as is

7. The marching bands <u>will arrive</u> soon.
   ○ will arrive   ○ will arrived   ○ correct as is

8. The floats <u>will shows</u> an old-time newspaper office.
   ○ will showed   ○ will show   ○ correct as is

9. When <u>will</u> the dancers <u>performed</u>?
   ○ will perform   ○ will performs   ○ correct as is

10. Tomorrow we <u>will celebrate</u> with a picnic.
    ○ will celebrates   ○ will celebrated   ○ correct as is

Past Continuous Tense

The **past continuous tense** refers to actions and events happening at a certain time in the past. We form the past continuous tense with **was/were** + **verb ending in -ing**.

Underline the verb in the past continuous tense in each sentence.

1. Reuben stayed at home all day because it was raining outside.

2. He was making his model airplane with his sister.

3. He was looking at the instructions on a piece of paper.

4. His sister was helping him to glue the pieces together.

5. His mother was cooking chicken for lunch.

6. She was glad the children were not arguing.

7. They were working together.

8. She was planning to reward them with ice cream after lunch.

Complete each sentence with the past continuous form of the verb in brackets.

9. Pete _____ (play) tennis at the tennis court.

10. He _____ (try) to hit the ball to the other side of the net.

11. The sun _____ (shine) brightly in the sky.

12. Sweat _____ (roll) down Pete's face.

13. He _____ (begin) to feel tired.

14. His friends _____ (cheer) for him.

© 2013 Scholastic Education International (S) Pte Ltd ISBN 978-981-07-5259-0

Past Continuous Tense

> We can use the **past continuous tense** and the **simple past tense** in the same sentence to describe an action that happened while another action was taking place.

Underline the past continuous tense of the verb in each sentence. Circle each simple past tense verb.

1. Joe was rushing out the door when he heard the telephone ring.

2. He was reaching for it when a crash came from the kitchen.

3. He was stepping into the kitchen when a cat dashed past him.

4. He was looking at the mess of broken plates when a car horn sounded outside.

5. He cut his finger while he was picking up the plates.

Complete each sentence with the past continuous tense of the verb in brackets.

6. The crowd _____ (cheer) when the team entered the stadium.

7. The school band _____ (play) a cheerful tune while the cheerleaders performed.

8. Everyone _____ (feel) a sense of excitement as they awaited the start of the game.

9. The mascots _____ (entertain) the children in the front row.

10. Poor little Sam _____ (cry) alone in the locker room.

Date: _____

Past Continuous Tense

Fill in the bubble next to the past continuous verb that correctly completes each sentence.

1. Many events _____ on at the same time at the funfair.
   ○ are going   ○ were going   ○ is going

2. I _____ cotton candy at the stall my class set up.
   ○ sold   ○ am selling   ○ was selling

3. Peter _____ to win a prize at the game stall.
   ○ tries   ○ was trying   ○ were trying

4. My cousins _____ themselves silly at the Haunted House.
   ○ were scared   ○ was scaring   ○ were scaring

5. All the while, loud music _____ from the speakers overhead.
   ○ blared   ○ was blaring   ○ were blaring

Complete each sentence using the past continuous tense of the verb in brackets and other words of your own.

6. When I entered the room, he _____

   _____. (read)

7. He did not hear me as I _____

   _____. (tiptoe)

8. The radio _____. (play)

   and he _____. (hum)

Main Verbs and Helping Verbs

> **Main verbs** show the main action in a sentence. **Helping verbs** help the main verb show tense. Helping verbs, such as **am**, **is**, **are**, **was**, **were**, **has**, **have**, **had** and **will**, work with main verbs to tell when an action occurs.

Read each sentence. Underline the helping verb and circle the main verb.

1. The guests will arrive very shortly.

2. Aunt Agatha has baked a whole tray of muffins.

3. Patty was cleaning the furniture.

4. Uncle Ike had repaired the spoilt lamps.

5. The rest of us were setting up the decorations.

Underline the helping verb and circle the main verb. Then, identify when the action occurs by writing *past, present* or *future* on the line.

6. The lady had asked for baking powder. _____

7. The rings of batter will drop into the hot fat. _____

8. Homer is learning about the doughnut machine. _____

9. People will enjoy the doughnuts later. _____

10. Everyone has eaten the doughnuts. _____

Main Verbs and Helping Verbs

Circle the answer in brackets that best completes each sentence.

1. Justin (was cooking / will cooking) seafood stew.

2. He (had added / is added) spices and lemon juice.

3. Sally and Mick (will prepared / have prepared) stew before.

4. Justin (is tasting / had tasting) the broth.

5. "I (will add / has add) a little more pepper," says Justin.

6. His friends (have arrived / are arrived) for dinner.

Write sentences using the main and helping verbs in brackets.

7. (will meet) _____

8. (had arrived) _____

9. (have heard) _____

10. (are eating) _____

11. (were sleeping) _____

Date: _____

Main Verbs and Helping Verbs

Decide if the underlined verb in each sentence is correct. If it is not, write the correct answer on the line.

1. Today Fran <u>will traveled</u> to Peru by plane.   _____

2. She <u>is photograph</u> the stone ruins of Machu
    Picchu next week.   _____

3. An American explorer <u>had discovered</u> the
    ancient city in 1911.   _____

4. Since then, many people <u>have visit</u> the ruins of the city.   _____

5. Yesterday, Fran's brothers <u>had looking</u> at pictures
    of Machu Picchu.   _____

6. They <u>was wondering</u> about the Inca civilization.   _____

Underline the helping verbs and write the main verbs on the lines.

7. On Saturday, Betty will bake rye bread.   _____

8. Henry has picked some cucumbers.   _____

9. Jim is picking raspberries and blackberries.   _____

10. Alison had planted a herb garden.   _____

11. Marie and Harry have tossed the salad.   _____

12. They are planning another picnic.   _____

Connectors

Connectors are joining words used to combine two or more words, phrases or sentences. Besides **and**, other connectors that show addition are **too**, **as well as**, **both … and**, and **not only … but also**.

Circle the connector(s) in each sentence that show addition. Underline the two words or phrases that are combined.

1. Jess wanted to go to the circus and the theme park.

2. Dad declared it would not be possible to visit the circus as well as the theme park.

3. He said it was not only too expensive, but also too time-consuming.

4. At either place, they would have to pay a lot for admission. The food there would be costly, too.

5. Both Dad and Mom agreed that Jess had to choose one or the other.

Combine each pair of sentences using the connector in brackets.

6. The elephants were led into the ring by their trainers. The horses were led into the ring by their trainers. (both)

   _____

7. The crowd loved the monkeys. The crowd loved the clowns. (as well as)

   _____

8. The flying trapeze act was thrilling. The flying trapeze act was entertaining. (not only … but also)

   _____

© 2013 Scholastic Education International (S) Pte Ltd ISBN 978-981-07-5259-0

Connectors

Besides **but**, other connectors that show contrast are **although**, **though**, **while**, **yet** and **however**.

Circle the connector(s) in each sentence that show contrast.

1. Will and Liam are twins, but they are not alike at all.

2. Although Will has a round face, Liam has an oval face.

3. Will has bushy brows while Liam's brows are thin and fine.

4. Will likes music though Liam prefers sports.

5. Will is good at Math, yet he does not write as well as Liam.

Combine each pair of sentences using the connector in brackets.

6. The toad and frog are both amphibians. They are different in many ways. (although)

_____

7. Frogs have long hind legs for leaping. Toads have short hind legs for walking. (but)

_____

8. Frogs have smooth or slimy skin. The skin of toads is warty and dry. (while)

_____

9. Frogs tend to lay eggs in clusters. Toads tend to lay eggs in long chains. (though)

_____

Assessment

Connectors

Fill in the bubble next to the connector that correctly completes each sentence.

1. It was a fine day, _____ there were surprisingly few people at the beach.
   - ○ however
   - ○ yet
   - ○ as well as

2. We planned to play beach volleyball _____ forgot to bring our ball.
   - ○ and
   - ○ but
   - ○ though

3. We _____ swam in the sea _____ built sandcastles.
   - ○ also ... too
   - ○ both ... also
   - ○ not only ... but also

4. _____ it was sunny in the morning, the sky began to darken in the afternoon.
   - ○ Not only
   - ○ Although
   - ○ However

5. We did not mind getting wet. _____, it was dangerous to play in a storm.
   - ○ However
   - ○ Though
   - ○ While

Fill in the bubble next to the words that best complete each sentence.

6. Ali owns a car as well as _____.
   - ○ he drives
   - ○ a motorcycle

7. Although the car is more comfortable, _____.
   - ○ Ali likes the car
   - ○ Ali rides the motorcycle to work

8. The car is not only faster on the highway, _____.
   - ○ but it is also safer
   - ○ although it is safer

9. While the motorcycle may be less comfortable, _____.
   - ○ it is useful in heavy traffic
   - ○ but it is useful in heavy traffic

88

More Connectors

> Some **connectors** show how actions or events are related in terms of time.

Underline the connector(s) in each sentence that show time relationships.

1. The audience clapped when the curtains opened on stage.

2. Before the emcee could speak, they cheered loudly.

3. She did not speak until the audience became quiet.

4. After welcoming them, she introduced the first concert item.

5. The dancers smiled as they twirled gracefully on the stage.

6. While the dancers performed, the musicians prepared themselves.

7. As soon as the curtains closed, they took up their positions on the stage.

Complete each sentence using a suitable time connector from the sentences above.

8. _____ the train stopped at the station, we jumped off happily.

9. _____ my cousin Mary saw us, she waved excitedly.

10. Dad had called her _____ our visit to arrange for her to meet us.

11. Mary said she had waited there _____ parking her car.

12. _____ we were on our way to Aunt Grace's house, we chatted with Mary non-stop.

More Connectors

Some **connectors** show the order or sequence in which actions or events take place.

Underline the connectors that tell the order or time in which the actions take place.

1. First, mix 2 eggs, 2 tablespoons of milk, and a dash of pepper or salt in a bowl.

2. Then, butter the frying pan.

3. Next, pour the egg mix onto the pan.

4. As the top sets, lift the top slightly to let the uncooked part flow under it.

5. When the omelet is set, remove the pan from the heat.

6. Then, sprinkle some cheese in the middle of the omelet.

7. After that, fold the cheese omelet in half and put it onto a plate.

Read these sentences. Underline the time connectors. Then, arrange the sentences in the correct order starting with 1 for the action that begins first.

8. _____ After cutting it out, fold the bottom of the alien.

9. _____ First, use superglue to stick the two CDs together to form a spaceship.

10. _____ When your alien is ready, glue it to the colored spaceship.

11. _____ Then, cut out the alien, leaving a bit at the bottom to fold up.

12. _____ Next, draw an alien on the colored paper with a marker.

Date: _____

More Connectors

Fill in the bubble next to the connector that correctly completes each sentence.

1. _____ Mom left for work, she gave Jenny a list of chores to do.
   ○ Until   ○ First   ○ Before

2. _____, Jenny placed the laundry in the washing machine.
   ○ After   ○ First   ○ When

3. _____ the clothes were in the wash, Jenny mopped the floor.
   ○ Before   ○ While   ○ Next

4. _____ the washing machine stopped, Jenny hung them to dry.
   ○ Until   ○ After   ○ Before

5. _____, Jenny fixed lunch for herself.
   ○ When   ○ Next   ○ While

6. She watched her favorite cartoon _____ she ate her lunch.
   ○ until   ○ as   ○ next

7. Mom was pleased, so Jenny had a huge ice cream to herself _____ dinner.
   ○ when   ○ while   ○ after

Write connectors on the lines to show the order of the steps in making French toast.

8. _____, beat the eggs and sugar together.

9. _____, dip a slice of bread into the mixture.

10. _____, melt butter in a frying pan and fry
    the bread.

Adverbs

An **adverb** is a word that describes a verb, an adjective, or another adverb. Some adverbs tell when or where something happens.

Underline the verb. Then, circle the adverb that tells when.

1. Later, newsboys shouted the weekend forecast.

2. That night, a huge snowstorm hit New York City.

3. A train tried to plow through the snow earlier.

4. Then, the train went off the track.

Underline the verb. Then, circle the adverb that tells where.

5. Snow fell everywhere.

6. People were trapped inside.

7. Some people tunneled out from their homes.

8. They built a shelter by the river.

Underline the adverb in each sentence. Write *when* if the adverb tells when or *where* if it tells where.

9. People had never seen a storm so bad. _____

10. Pipes burst underground. _____

11. The water inside had frozen. _____

12. Soon people started to freeze, too. _____

© 2013 Scholastic Education International (S) Pte Ltd ISBN 978-981-07-5259-0

Adverbs

An **adverb** is a word that describes a verb, an adjective or another adverb. Some adverbs tell how. Many adverbs that tell how end in **–ly**.

Underline the verb and circle the adverb that describes it and tells how.

1. Grandma talked happily to the sea lions.

2. The seabirds squawked sharply as they dived.

3. Andy greeted the girl and Grandma warmly.

4. He guided them expertly through the islands.

5. The girl recorded the trip faithfully in her diary.

6. They looked eagerly at the creatures on the show.

7. Grandma and the girl jumped quickly off the boat.

8. They snorkeled easily with their tubes and fins.

9. The girl saw sea creatures clearly through her face mask.

10. She gazed intently at the yellow-tailed surgeonfish.

11. Swiftly the sea lions surrounded Grandma and the girl.

Complete each sentence with an action verb and an adverb that describes it and tells how.

12. The big male sea lion _____.

13. The girl and her grandmother _____.

Date: _____

Adverbs

Fill in the bubble next to the adverb that tells how.

1. Carolina and Gabriella dove rapidly under a big wave.
    - ○ rapidly
    - ○ under
    - ○ big

2. Then, a wave crashed loudly against the shore.
    - ○ crashed
    - ○ loudly
    - ○ against

3. Both Carolina and Gabriella were very strong swimmers.
    - ○ Both
    - ○ very
    - ○ strong

4. At the beach, the tide was somewhat low.
    - ○ beach
    - ○ low
    - ○ somewhat

5. Carolina quickly spotted a group of dolphins.
    - ○ quickly
    - ○ spotted
    - ○ group

Fill in the bubble next to the word that is not an adverb.

6. Carolina and Gabriella swam very slowly towards the playful mammals.
    - ○ swam
    - ○ slowly
    - ○ playful

7. "They are so curious!" Carolina exclaimed excitedly.
    - ○ so
    - ○ curious
    - ○ excitedly

8. One baby dolphin came very close.
    - ○ One
    - ○ very
    - ○ close

9. The mother dolphin nudged Carolina so gently.
    - ○ nudged
    - ○ so
    - ○ gently

10. Then, swiftly and mysteriously, the dolphins disappeared.
    - ○ swiftly
    - ○ disappeared
    - ○ mysteriously

More Adverbs

An **adverb** describes a verb, an adjective or another adverb. Some adverbs tell when or how often an action or event takes place.

Underline the adverbs that tell when. Circle the adverbs that tell how often.

1. Yesterday, Joe took his cat to the vet to groom its fur.

2. He has to do this monthly or its fur will be all knotted up.

3. He takes good care of his cat, feeding and playing with it daily.

4. Usually, he gives it cat food from the pet shop.

5. Occasionally, he gives it some salmon as a treat.

6. He never forgets to feed the cat.

7. Sometimes, when he is sick or busy, he asks his mum to help him.

8. It always leaps into Joe's arms when he comes home.

Complete each sentence with a suitable adverb that has the same meaning as the words in brackets.

9. Mrs Smith is _____ on time for class, because she does not like to be late. (all the time)

10. She walks to and from school _____. (every day)

11. _____, when it rains, she takes the longer way under shelter. (at times)

12. But _____, she walks along the riverside. (most of the time)

13. She makes a stop at the post office _____ to pay her bills. (once a month)

More Adverbs

An **adverb** describes a verb, an adjective or another adverb. Some adverbs also tell how long an action or event lasts.

Underline the adverbs that tell when, how long or how often. Circle the verb that the adverb describes.

1. Samy's dad often travels to other cities on business.

2. He usually goes to Hong Kong, but sometimes to Bangkok too.

3. He makes about four trips monthly.

4. He seldom comes home without bringing Samy a gift.

5. But Samy does not always like the gifts he gets.

6. Yesterday, his dad gave him some deep-fried crickets to taste.

7. Samy took one look at them and ran out of the room immediately.

8. Early this morning, his dad left for Hong Kong.

9. Samy hopes he will bring home some yummy cookies soon.

10. Samy's dad seldom disappoints him.

Complete each sentence with an adverb you underlined above. It should have the same meaning as the words in brackets.

11. Sylvia visited the dentist _____. (day before today)

12. She _____ visits the dentist, so there was a lot for the dentist to do. (not often)

13. Her father _____ visits the dentist. (frequently)

Date: _____

More Adverbs

Fill in the bubble next to the verb that the underlined adverb describes.

1. Frankie works out at the nearby gym <u>weekly</u>.
   ○ Frankie   ○ works   ○ nearby

2. He <u>hardly</u> misses his visit to the gym.
   ○ misses   ○ visit   ○ gym

3. He also jogs <u>frequently</u> in the park in the evenings.
   ○ also   ○ jogs   ○ evenings

4. <u>Sometimes</u>, his wife joins him on his evening jog.
   ○ wife   ○ joins   ○ jog

5. She stops <u>briefly</u> to chat with the neighbors at the park.
   ○ stops   ○ chat   ○ neighbors

Fill in the bubble next to the adverb that tells when, how often or how long.

6. Mom is going to cook pasta for dinner _____.
   ○ deliciously   ○ tonight   ○ neighbors

7. She _____ cooks dinner because she usually gets home late from work.
   ○ seldom   ○ enjoys   ○ lovingly

8. My cousin is staying over at our place _____.
   ○ temporarily   ○ fortunately   ○ noisily

9. Mom _____ makes special effort to cook for him whenever he stays over.
   ○ likes   ○ always   ○ daily

Infinitives

An **infinitive** is the base form of a verb. It usually comes after modal verbs and the helping verbs **do** and **have**, for example, **may go**, **did not go**.

Underline the infinitive in each sentence.

1. Jamie did not feel well this morning.

2. She could not get out of bed by herself.

3. Her parents had to take her to a doctor at the clinic.

4.. The doctor said that they should take her to the hospital.

5. He said she might have dengue fever.

6. At the hospital, the doctor said they would have to keep her overnight for tests.

7. Jamie's mom will stay at the hospital with her tonight.

8. I may visit her later this afternoon.

9. I am sure she will get well soon.

10. Her parents must be quite worried.

Complete each sentence with a suitable infinitive.

11. We must _____ up a good show for Drama Night this year.

12. We should _____ together as a class.

13. If anyone has any good ideas for a plot, could you _____ me, please.

14. Please do not _____ afraid to share any ideas you have.

15. I am sure you will _____ your parents proud when they come to watch you perform.

Infinitives

An **infinitive** is the base form of a verb. We often add *to* in front of the infinitive to form the **to-infinitive**, for example, ***to run***.

Underline the to-infinitive in each sentence.

1. Jane is at the market with Grandma to buy some fresh food.

2. Grandma has planned to prepare many dishes for Jane's party tonight.

3. She learned to cook from her own mother when she was young.

4. Jane wanted to order pizza, but Grandma would not let her.

5. Grandma wants to teach Jane how to choose fresh ingredients.

6. She expects Jane to watch her and help her as she cooks.

7. She asked Jane to eat less fast food.

8. She told Jane to watch her diet and to take more vegetables.

Complete each sentence with a suitable infinitive.

9. There are a few more guests who have yet to _____ at the party.

10. Many friends have come to _____ Jane's birthday.

11. They are amazed to _____ the many dishes on the table.

12. They cannot wait to _____ eating.

Date: _____

Infinitives

Read each sentence. Fill in the bubble next to the word that is an infinitive.

1. Dad took my brother and me to watch a soccer game last night.
   - ○ took
   - ○ watch
   - ○ game

2. We wanted to get good seats, so we went early.
   - ○ wanted
   - ○ get
   - ○ went

3. Although we were not at the grandstand, we could see well from our seats.
   - ○ were
   - ○ could
   - ○ see

4. Dad explained the game because we did not know the rules.
   - ○ explained
   - ○ did
   - ○ know

5. I can explain the rules of the game now to you if you like.
   - ○ can
   - ○ explain
   - ○ like

Fill in the bubble next to the infinitive verb that completes each sentence.

6. I love to _____ out of the window during a storm.
   - ○ look
   - ○ looking
   - ○ looks

7. I can _____ the trees bending over in the strong wind.
   - ○ saw
   - ○ sees
   - ○ see

8. The sky will _____ up when lightning flashes.
   - ○ lit
   - ○ light
   - ○ lights

9. The roar of thunder will _____ soon after.
   - ○ follow
   - ○ follows
   - ○ following

10. I like to _____ the splashes the rain makes on the ground.
    - ○ watching
    - ○ watch
    - ○ watches

Date: _____

Contractions

> A **contraction** is two words written as one word. We use an apostrophe in place of the missing letter or letters.
> Example: **I will** eat some biscuits.
> **I'll** eat some biscuits.

Read each sentence. Underline the contraction. Write the two words the contraction is made from.

1. She'll be here any minute.   _____ _____

2. You'd better get ready soon.   _____ _____

3. She doesn't like to wait.   _____ _____

4. Don't you want to bring more money?   _____ _____

5. You're sure this is enough?   _____ _____

Draw a line to match each contraction with the two words it is made from.

6. I'll   are not

7. aren't   I will / I shall

8. wouldn't   shall not

9. shan't   would not

10. won't   will not

11. we'll   it is

12. it's   we will

© 2013 Scholastic Education International (S) Pte Ltd ISBN 978-981-07-5259-0

Contractions

Read each sentence. Write a contraction for the underlined words.

1. <u>They are</u> going to the party tonight.   _____

2. <u>I will</u> be going with them.   _____

3. Marge <u>is not</u> sure if she can make it tonight.   _____

4. Jack said that <u>he had</u> agreed to be the host.   _____

5. <u>I am</u> looking forward to the party.   _____

6. <u>You are</u> going to be there, aren't you?   _____

Write sentences using the contractions in brackets.

7. (you'll) _____

8. (it's) _____

9. (wouldn't) _____

10. (mustn't) _____

11. (he'd) _____

Assessment

Contractions

Write a contraction for the underlined words.

1. <u>They will</u> see the project through to the end.   _____

2. You <u>must not</u> give up halfway.   _____

3. It is important to complete what <u>you have</u> started.   _____

4. <u>We have</u> a long way to go.   _____

5. <u>It is</u> time to get down to work.   _____

Fill in the bubble next to the contraction that correctly completes the sentence.

6. Patsy _____ a very big cat but she is fierce.

    ○ aren't   ○ isn't   ○ haven't

7. _____ very good at chasing mice.

    ○ She's   ○ She'll   ○ She'd

8. _____ play with her toys in the afternoon.

    ○ She's   ○ She'll   ○ You're

9. _____ very proud of my cat.

    ○ I'll   ○ I'd   ○ I'm

10. Patsy knows she _____ disturb the fish in the tank.

    ○ mustn't   ○ won't   ○ hadn't

© 2013 Scholastic Education International (S) Pte Ltd   ISBN 978-981-07-5259-0

Direct Speech

> **Direct speech** shows exactly what a speaker says. We use **quotation marks** to show the beginning and end of the speaker's exact words.

Read each sentence. Add the missing punctuation marks to each sentence.

1. _____ I am a big fan of hers _____ _____ replied Sharon.

2. I added _____ _____ Sally can even sing a wolf to sleep _____ _____

3. _____ How did Sally tame King Bear _____ _____ asked our teacher.

4. _____ Sally ought to be in the movies _____ _____ said Don.

5. _____ What kind of person is Sally _____ _____ asked Davy.

6. The man replied _____ _____ Sally is a special friend _____ _____

7. _____ She can laugh the bark off a tree _____ _____ added Lucy _____

8. The man said _____ _____ She can dance a rock to pieces _____ _____

9. _____ I'm very impressed _____ _____ exclaimed Davy _____

Write two sentences of dialogue to continue the conversation above.

10. _____.

11. _____.

© 2013 Scholastic Education International (S) Pte Ltd ISBN 978-981-07-5259-0

Date: _____

Direct Speech

> **Quotation marks** show a speaker's exact words. **Commas** set off introductory words, such as **oh**, **thank you**, **yes**, **no** and **well**, and the name of the person who is being addressed.

Add the missing commas to the sentences.

1. "Well ____ we are having a food drive next week."

2. "Oh ____ Ed ____ can you bring some containers to school?"

3. "Yes ____ I have several at home, Jody."

4. "Thank you ____ Mr Poole, for all your suggestions."

Add the missing quotation marks and /or commas to each sentence.

5. ____ Kim, your posters for the talent contest are terrific! ____ I exclaimed.

6. She replied, ____ Thank you. ____

7. Our teacher asked, ____ Meg ____ will you play your guitar or sing? ____

8. "Oh ____ I plan to do both, ____ said Meg.

9. ____ Will you be juggling this year ____ Robert? ____ Jay asked.

10. ____ No ____ I want to do a comedy routine, ____ he replied.

Write two sentences of dialogue about a school talent show.

11. _____.

12. _____.

Date: _____

Direct Speech

Rewrite each sentence correctly.

1. "Rosa, tell me a joke" said Ken.

    _____

2. "What years do frogs like best. asked Rosa.

    _____

3. "Frogs like Hoppy New Years! Laughed Ken.

    _____

4. "No frogs like leap years?"said Rosa.

    _____

5. "Oh that was funny!" exclaimed Ken.

    _____

6. I like your joke too, said Rosa.

    _____

7. "Do you have any more jokes." asked Ken.

    _____

Indirect Speech

> We use **indirect speech** to report what a person has said. If the speech contains a **present tense verb**, we often change it to the **past tense**. We often need to change the **pronouns** too.

Underline the verbs that we should change to the past tense when we convert the direct speech into indirect speech. Write the past tense verb or verbs on the line.

1. "Tom loves the ice cream," said Hakim. _____

2. "He likes the chocolates too," added Judy. _____

Underline the pronouns that we should change when we convert the direct speech into indirect speech. Write the new pronoun on the line.

3. "He does not know we are going to visit him," said Tracy. _____

4. "We will surprise him with chocolate ice cream!" exclaimed Hakim. _____

Rewrite these sentences as indirect speech.

5. "I can buy the ice cream on my way to Tom's house," Tracy said.

_____

6. "I will bring the birthday card along," Hakim added.

_____

7. "I'm sure he will have a pleasant surprise," Judy said.

_____

Indirect Speech

> We use **indirect speech** to report what a person has said. If the speech contains a past tense verb, we often change it to the **past perfect**. We often need to change the **pronouns** and **adverbials** too.

Compare each pair of sentences in direct and indirect speech. Underline the words that have been changed in each sentence.

1. "I went to France last year," Grace told me.

    Grace told me that she had gone to France the previous year.

2. "I can still remember how many steps we climbed to get to the top of the Eiffel Tower," she said.

    She said that she could still remember how many steps they had climbed to get to the top of the Eiffel Tower.

3. "What I really loved were the desserts," she added.

    She added that what she had really loved had been the desserts.

Rewrite these sentences as indirect speech.

4. "I asked you to discuss your vacation plans for this summer," Miss Henny told the girls.

    _____

    _____

5. "I did not tell you to talk about what you did last summer," she added.

    _____

    _____

 © 2013 Scholastic Education International (S) Pte Ltd ISBN 978-981-07-5259-0

Assessment

Date: _____

Indirect Speech

Fill in the bubble next to the word that needs to be changed for indirect speech.

1. "We shall begin this meeting with the place for the picnic," Sonny announced.
   ○ We   ○ begin   ○ announced

2. "The zoo has a nice picnic ground," Susan suggested.
   ○ suggested   ○ has   ○ nice

3. "We went to the zoo for our picnic last year," Hans complained.
   ○ complained   ○ zoo   ○ last

4. "There is a cool picnic area near the beach too," said Susan.
   ○ is   ○ near   ○ too

5. "I think the beach is a good idea," Sonny said.
   ○ beach   ○ good   ○ I

Fill in the bubble next to the correct word change for indirect speech.

6. "We will now discuss what to bring for the picnic," announced Sonny.
   ○ will → shall   ○ We → They   ○ bring → take

7. "I can pack some sandwiches for everyone," offered Sally.
   ○ pack → make   ○ offered → offers   ○ I → She

8. "I can bring packet drinks," said Su Mei.
   ○ I → They   ○ can → could   ○ drinks → food

9. "We did not have enough to drink last year," said Hans.
   ○ We → You   ○ did → had   ○ enough → much

10. "You are always complaining," Sonny told Hans.
    ○ You → I   ○ are → was   ○ always → never

Prepositions of Time and Position

Prepositions tell us how a noun or pronoun relates to another. Some prepositions give information about position.

Underline the preposition in each sentence that gives information on position.

1. We have just moved into our new house on Elim Street.

2. There is so much to do around the house.

3. Dad is fixing the lamp above the dining table.

4. Mom wants us to check that the cabinets are against the walls.

5. That way, tiny insects cannot hide behind the cabinets.

6. I like the patio outside the house.

7. Mom plans to plant a row of herbs along the side of the patio.

8. There is a narrow row between our house and my neighbor's house.

Circle the correct preposition to complete each sentence.

9. Thousands of asteroids streak (on / in / past) Earth every year.

10. Some land (on / in / above) Earth as meteorites.

11. In 2013, a huge meteorite landed (on / in / past) a Russian city.

12. The meteor broke apart (over / under / between) Russia with a huge boom that shook buildings and broke windows.

© 2013 Scholastic Education International (S) Pte Ltd ISBN 978-981-07-5259-0

Prepositions of Time and Position

Some **prepositions** give information about position and some tell about time.

Underline the preposition in each sentence and write *time* or *position* on the line to indicate the type of preposition.

1. I met Joseph during the school holidays. _____

2. Joseph was riding his bicycle when he saw me. _____

3. He stopped beside the sidewalk and we chatted briefly. _____

4. He had a basket behind him, where his puppy sat. _____

5. I played with his puppy for a few minutes. _____

Fill in the bubble next to the preposition that best completes the sentence.

6. The boys were tired, but they knew they were _____ their destination.
   ○ on   ○ in   ○ near

7. They had been hiking _____ more than four hours and were tired.
   ○ for   ○ during   ○ at

8. The final checkpoint had to be _____ the bushes marked by 'X' on the map.
   ○ above   ○ among   ○ down

9. Sure enough, Tim picked up the familiar red ball and raised it triumphantly _____ his head.
   ○ on   ○ above   ○ in

10. They had successfully completed the quest _____ dark.
    ○ in   ○ during   ○ before

Date: _____

Prepositions of Time and Position

Circle the correct preposition to complete each sentence.

1. In March 2011, a huge wave that started out (on / above / in) the ocean swept onto the coast of Japan.

2. It carried away everything (on / past / in) its path.

3. (In / For / After) more than a year, a soccer ball and a volleyball washed up off the coast of Alaska.

4. The man who found them sent them back to the teenager who lost them (on / during / for) the tsunami.

5. He was walking (along / behind / above) the beach when he found the balls.

6. The messages written (above / on / among) the ball helped him to find the owners.

Fill in the bubble next to the preposition that best completes the sentence.

7. Researchers suspected that there was a famous mural on a wall _____ another mural in Italy last year.

    ○ behind   ○ in   ○ before

8. They put a probe with a camera _____ it through the first mural by Vasari.

    ○ on   ○ during   ○ among

9. _____ the first mural, they found the famous painting by Da Vinci.

    ○ Above   ○ Underneath   ○ After

10. They believe that Vasari created another painting _____ Leonardo's painting.

    ○ in   ○ over   ○ in front of

© 2013 Scholastic Education International (S) Pte Ltd ISBN 978-981-07-5259-0

Prepositions of Direction

Prepositions tell us how a noun or pronoun relates to another. Some prepositions give information about how a person or thing moves in relation to another. They are called **prepositions of direction**.

Underline the preposition(s) of direction in each sentence.

1. The acrobats who performed that evening came from China.

2. Some entered by somersaulting across the stage.

3. Others cartwheeled from the back of the stage towards the audience.

4. They also did some well-timed leapfrogging, where one would jump over another.

5. We were amazed to see a child jumping through hoops that were on fire.

6. Their movements were timed precisely, and they leapt and rolled past one another smoothly.

Write complete sentences using the given words and a suitable preposition from above to show movement and direction.

7. The waves ... rolled ... the sea

   _____

8. Roger watched ... binoculars

   _____

9. He saw ... dog ... running ... man

   _____

10 The man threw ... stick ... beach

   _____

Prepositions of Direction

Circle the correct preposition to complete each sentence.

1. The driver of the red car was impatient to get (through / in) the heavy traffic.

2. He veered right suddenly to move (over / out of) his lane.

3. He wanted to overtake the bus and zoom (past / over) it.

4. A motorcycle appeared in the right lane (in / from) the back.

5. The motorcyclist was moving (to / towards) the red car at a high speed.

6. He could not stop in time and rammed (past / into) the red car.

7. He vaulted (under / over) the car and landed on the road.

8. Many drivers and pedestrians gathered (through / around) the scene of the accident.

Write three sentences about an accident in school using any of the above prepositions of direction.

9. _____

    _____

10. _____

    _____

11. _____

    _____

© 2013 Scholastic Education International (S) Pte Ltd ISBN 978-981-07-5259-0

Assessment

Date: _____

Prepositions of Direction

Fill in the bubble next to the preposition that correctly completes the sentence.

1. The obstacle course stood _____ the boys and the challenge trophy.
    ○ on   ○ in   ○ between

2. First, they crawled _____ a wire mesh on muddy ground.
    ○ between   ○ up   ○ under

3. Then, they balanced on a log to get _____ a wide drain.
    ○ through   ○ across   ○ along

4. Next, they crawled _____ a pitch-dark underground tunnel.
    ○ through   ○ past   ○ between

5. Finally, they climbed _____ a high wall with the help of our teammates.
    ○ into   ○ over   ○ on

Circle the preposition that correctly completes the sentence.

6. Roy was taking a leisurely stroll (into / along / over) the road bordering the city park.

7. Suddenly, he saw a soccer ball flying (into / onto / towards) him.

8. He tried to avoid it and stepped (into / over / through) a puddle of muddy water.

9. To his dismay, the ball landed in another puddle nearby and splashed mud (into / onto / through) him.

10. Two children who were walking (past / along / over) Roy sniggered at him.

Revision

Fill in the bubble next to the name for the noun that is underlined.

1. The <u>International Olympic Committee (IOC)</u> is planning to drop wrestling from the 2020 Summer Games.

   ○ common noun   ○ proper noun   ○ collective noun

2. <u>Wrestling</u> is an ancient sport, dating back to the very first modern Olympics in Athens, Greece, in 1896.

   ○ common noun   ○ proper noun   ○ collective noun

3. U.S. wrestling <u>coach</u> Zeke Jones said the sport is bringing the people of the U.S. and Iran closer together.

   ○ common noun   ○ proper noun   ○ collective noun

4. The American <u>team</u> is in Iran for a wrestling tournament.

   ○ common noun   ○ proper noun   ○ collective noun

Fill in the bubble next to the pronoun that correctly completes the sentence.

5. The wolf found it difficult to catch the sheep because _____ were well protected by the shepherd.

   ○ it   ○ he   ○ they

6. The wolf knew that the shepherd always keeps a lookout for _____.

   ○ him   ○ he   ○ his

7. One day, he found the skin of a sheep, so he put it over _____.

   ○ him   ○ himself   ○ it

© 2013 Scholastic Education International (S) Pte Ltd ISBN 978-981-07-5259-0

8. Then, he walked towards the sheep and lured one of _____ away from the shepherd.

   ○ they   ○ their   ○ them

Fill in the bubble next to the article or quantifier that correclty completes the sentence.

9. Harris is a poor and homeless man, who has _____ money and sometimes sleeps under a bridge.

   ○ much   ○ no   ○ many

10. There is _____ cup next to him, in which passersby may put their spare change.

   ○ a   ○ an   ○ the

11. Occasionally, someone would drop _____ coins into his cup.

   ○ a little   ○ fewer   ○ a few

12. Recently, a young lady stopped and poured _____ her change from her purse into his cup.

   ○ little   ○ some   ○ all

Fill in the bubble next to the verb that correctly completes the sentence.

13. When the giant tortoise, Lonesome George, died in 2012, people _____ he was the last of his kind.

   ○ think   ○ thinks   ○ thought

14. He belonged to a species on Pinta Island not _____ anywhere else in the world.

   ○ find   ○ found   ○ founded

15. So, when he died, scientists believed the species had _____ extinct.

   ○ become   ○ becomes   ○ became

16. Now, a group of researchers _____ giant tortoises living on another island, Isabella Island.

   ○ find   ○ has found   ○ is finding

© 2013 Scholastic Education International (S) Pte Ltd ISBN 978-981-07-5259-0

17. These giant tortoises _____ be related to Lonesome George, according to the scientists who studied their DNA.

○ may   ○ will   ○ can

18. Scientists think that some of Lonesome George's species _____ be found in the Galapagos Islands.

○ can   ○ shall   ○ might

19. They plan to go there in the spring to _____ for them.

○ look   ○ looked   ○ looking

Circle the adjective that correctly completes the sentence.

20. A cave chief named Wu had two wives, one of whom died leaving a (loving / lovely) baby, Yeh-Shen.

21. Yeh-Shen's stepmother did not like her as she was (more beautiful / beautiful) and kinder than her own daughter.

22. Hence, she gave Yeh-Shen the (worse / worst) jobs in the house.

23. The only friend Yeh-Shen had was a fish with (big, golden round / golden, round big) eyes.

24. Her stepmother killed the fish and cooked it for dinner, causing Yeh-Shen to be (depressed / depressing).

25. As she sat crying, she heard a voice and looked up to see a (wise old small / small wise old) man before her.

26. He told her that the fish bones were filled with a (powered / powerful) spirit that could grant her wishes.

Fill in the bubble next to the adverb that correctly completes each sentence.

27. Very _____, the bell would ring for the last time for the term.

○ soonly   ○ soon   ○ often

28. The students were _____ packing their bags and files.

○ hurried   ○ hurriedly   ○ hurry

© 2013 Scholastic Education International (S) Pte Ltd ISBN 978-981-07-5259-0

29. _____, at this time, the teachers would say good-bye by distributing cards or gifts.

○ Usually   ○ Usual   ○ Never

30. However, Miss Sarah looked at them _____ and they knew something was wrong.

○ sad   ○ sadly   ○ sadness

31. She was always cheerful and bubbly, and they had _____ seen her looking so upset.

○ often   ○ never   ○ usually

Fill in the bubble next to the connector that correctly completes the sentence.

32. Margie was furious _____ she had to mind her little brother again.

○ but   ○ because   ○ until

33. _____ she quite liked him, today there was something much more exciting happening.

○ Although   ○ Even   ○ However

34. The boys were preparing to go on a hunt _____ they had not gone on any outings for months.

○ while   ○ after   ○ because

35. Her mother was out getting groceries, _____ Margie had to stay home to watch Didi.

○ so   ○ since   ○ such

36. She thought hard about what she could do to join the boys _____ they were getting ready.

○ while   ○ but   ○ and

Answer Key

Page 5
1. declarative 2. interrogative 3. imperative
4. imperative 5. exclamatory 6. incomplete
7. complete 8. complete 9. incomplete
Accept all reasonable answers.

Page 6
1. ? 2. ! 3. . 4. .
5. listened, declarative 6. play, interrogative
7. pass, imperative 8. won, declarative
Accept all reasonable answers.

Page 7
1. Do you like 2. Middle Ages.
3. correct as is 4. your life?
5. correct as is 6. in the ocean!
7. correct as is 8. Tell me another story
9. the sea. 10. his trip.

Page 8
1. Where 2. Who 3. When
4. What 5. Whose 6. When
7. Where 8. Who 9. What
10. When

Page 9
1. Which 2. Why 3. Which
4. How 5. Why
6. Which box did you buy?
7. Why did you buy the pink box?
8. What is she going to do with the box?
9. Where will she put the box?

Page 10
1. Where 2. What 3. When
4. Who 5. How 6. Which
7. Whose 8. Why

Page 11
1. Underline: A small family; Circle: family
2. Underline: The two children; Circle: children
3. Underline: The little girl; Circle: girl
4. Underline: Huge spaceships; Circle: spaceships
5. Underline: The spaceship mechanics;
   Circle: mechanics
6. Underline: Twinkling stars; Circle: stars
7. Underline: lived underground; Circle: lived

8. Underline: manufactures air inside their homes;
   Circle: manufactures
9. Underline: jumped into the air; Circle: jumped
10. Underline: cluttered the playroom; Circle: cluttered
11. Underline: described the weather; Circle: described

Page 12
1. We / watched the space shuttle on TV this morning.
2. The huge spaceship / rocketed into space at 6:00 a.m.
3. During the flight, the six astronauts / released a satellite into space.
4. The space shuttle *Columbia* / circled Earth for three days.
5. The spacecraft / landed smoothly on Monday.
6. The astronauts / came back to a hero's welcome.
Accept all reasonable answers.

Page 13
1. complete subject 2. complete predicate
3. simple subject 4. complete predicate
5. complete subject 6. simple predicate
7. simple subject 8. simple predicate
9. complete subject 10. complete predicate

Page 14
1. Underline: Laura and Ramona; Circle: and
2. Underline: Pa, Ma and Laura; Circle: and
3. Underline: The dog and horses; Circle: and
4. Underline: Ma and Pa; Circle: and
5. Underline: trees and bushes; Circle: or
6. Underline: swayed and creaked; Circle: and
7. Underline: hummed and sang; Circle: and
8. Underline: twisted and turned; Circle: and
9. Underline: neighed and snorted; Circle: and
10. Underline: stopped and stared; Circle: and
Accept all reasonable answers.

Page 15
Ensure that the compound subject (CS) and compound predicate (CP) is underlined correctly.
1. Underline: Mike and Jody (CS)
2. Underline: call or e-mail (CP)
3. Underline: jogs and swims (CP)
4. Underline: Phil and Jan (CS)
5. Underline: Juan and Yoshi (CS)
6. Underline: speak and read (CP)

© 2013 Scholastic Education International (S) Pte Ltd ISBN 978-981-07-5259-0

7. Underline: Lori, Sam and Beth (CS)
8. Underline: practiced and presented (CP)
9. Underline: clapped and smiled (CP)
10. Underline: parents and teachers (CS)
11. barked and jumped   12. My dad and sister

Page 16
1. compound subject   2. compound predicate
3. compound subject   4. compound predicate
5. compound subject   6. Paul and Annie
7. teachers and students 8. wrote and proofread
9. stamped and mailed
10. ran, skipped and jumped

Page 17
1. Underline: farmer, house, road
2. Underline: name; Circle: John Timus
3. Underline: farm; Circle: Rising J Horse Ranch
4. Underline: wheat, soybeans, corn; Circle: Mr Timus
5. Underline: fields, crops
6. Underline: crops, rows; Circle: Mr Timus
7. Underline: plants, weeds, bugs; Circle: Mr Timus
8. Underline: people; Circle: October, Timus Farm, Harvest Celebration
Accept all reasonable answers.

Page 18

Common Nouns	Proper Nouns
newspaper, day, city, book, magazine, month	The Sun News, July, Cobblestone, Chicago, Tuesday, Young Arthur

Accept all reasonable answers.

Page 19
1. I go to Stanfordshire Elementary School.
2. I brought a peanut butter sandwich.
3. We sang "Somewhere Over the Rainbow" today.
4. My school is located at the intersection of Maple Avenue and Elm Street.
5. My best friend John sits in the third row.
6. My favorite singer is Tina Bell.
7. I wrote a report about Beijing in China.
8. I did research on the Great Wall of China.

Page 20
1. Underline: door, cap, bat, game; Circle: shoes
2. Underline: field, bat, shoulder
3. Underline: fence; Circle: friends
4. Underline: baseball; Circle: friends
5. Circle: uncles, feet
6. Underline: bat; Circle: hands

7. Underline: ball; Circle: bases
8. Underline: team, day   9. stories
10. princesses   11. monsters   12. classes

Page 21
1. mice   2. men   3. children
4. teeth   5. feet   6. oxen
7. geese   8. deer   9. sheep
10. people   11. people   12. children
13. teeth   14. feet   15. stories

Page 22
1. chapters   2. sons   3. trees
4. nuts   5. cubs   6. bushes
7. berries   8. deer   9. foxes
10. tooth

Page 23
2. Underline: drawers; Circle: chest
3. Underline: beads; Circle: string
4. Underline: clean laundry; Circle: pile
5. Underline: kittens; Circle: litter
6. Underline: stamps; Circle: collection
7. Underline: stamp albums; Circle: stack
8. Underline: players; Circle: team
9. Underline: spectators; Circle: crowd
10. Underline: insects; Circle: swarm
11. stack   12. bunch   13. collection
14. litter   15. crowd

Page 24
1. gaggle   2. brood   3. troop
4. herd   5. flock   6. swarms
7. nest   8. litter   9. eggs
10. bread   11. bananas   12. grapes
13. flowers   14. cutlery

Page 25
1. team   2. fleet   3. flight
4. crowd   5. band   6. clump
7. pile   8. crate   9. wad
10. pack

Page 26
1. "I have a strange case," said Mr Brown.
2. "What's strange about it?" asked Jet.
3. "Mr Hunt found an elephant," said Mr Brown.
4. "It simply appeared in his window," said Mr Brown.
5. "He must have fainted!" exclaimed Jet.
6. "No, he bought it," said Mr Brown.
7. "What shall we do this afternoon?" asked James.
8. Peter replied, "Shall we go fishing?"
9. "Fishing is boring!" exclaimed James.

10. "Let's go skating instead," said Ian.
11. "Mum, may we go out today?" asked the boys.
12. Mum said, "Only after you finish your work."

Page 27
1. Mrs Wu's bank is at 92 Maple Avenue, Texas.
2. She opened an account there on August 8, 2012.
3. She also goes to the branch in Lakewood, Texas.
4. That branch opens on weekdays, Saturdays and some evenings.
5. The main office is closed on Saturdays, Sundays and holidays.
6. She saw Adam, Joan and Miss Clark at the bank.
7. She asked, "Where would you like me to put this?"
8. "You can put it on the table," replied Jon.
9. "Please leave the carrots, onions, potatoes and eggs in the fridge," said Jon.
10. "Then, send these to 12 Marsh Cross, Alabama," said Mr Jones.

Page 28
1. Patty asked, "What book did you all read?"
2. "We read a book called *At the Zoo*," said Mark.
3. "It had pictures of a lion, monkeys and bears," added Brent.
4. "It was fascinating!" said Mark.
5. "Can we go to the animal show?" asked Ben.
6. "Where is the show going to be?" asked Patty.
7. "The show will be at the Montry Zoo," said Ben.

Page 29
1. Who   2. What   3. Whose
4. Which   5. Who
6. What are you trying to repair?
7. Whose toy car is it?
8. Which brother are you talking about?
9. Who bought it for him?

Page 30
1. This   2. That   3. these
4. those   5. that   6. this
7. these   8. These   9. Those
10. that   11. That   12. those

Page 31
1. What   2. Who   3. Which
4. What   5. Who   6. this
7. This   8. those   9. that
10. these

Page 32
1. We   2. It   3. I   4. She   5. He
6. They   7. You   8. He   9. She   10. They
11. It   12. We

Page 33
1. us   2. it   3. him   4. you   5. me
6. her   7. them   8. them   9. her   10. it
11. him   12. us

Page 34
1. us   2. It   3. She   4. her   5. them
6. They   7. He   8. We   9. him   10. us

Page 35
1. Underline: my; Circle: yours
2. Underline: her; Circle: hers
3. Underline: his; Circle: his
4. Underline: their; Circle: ours
5. Underline: your; Circle: mine
6. Underline: our; Circle: theirs
7. My   8. their   9. her   10. his   11. their

Page 36
1. our   2. her   3. their   4. my   5. yours
6. theirs
7. His favorite food is apple pie.
8. The box of toy cars is theirs.
9. The white milk bowl belongs to our pet.
10. My friends said that this is their favorite dish.

Page 37
1. my   2. their   3. his
4. mine   5. our   6. ours
7. their   8. our   9. ours
10. her

Page 38
1. some   2. a few   3. many
4. no   5. no   6. any
7. many   8. Some   9. a lot of
10. any   11. No   12. many
13. A few, a lot of   14. none

Page 39
1. many   2. a little   3. a few
4. some   5. a little   6. much
7. a few   8. any   9. many
10. some   11. Some   12. a few
13. no   14. any   15. a few

Page 40
1. much   2. a lot of   3. a few
4. Some   5. little   6. a little
7. much   8. no   9. a few
10. any

122

Page 41

1. more
2. fewer
3. more
4. fewer
5. less
6. fewer
7. fewer
8. more
9. more
10. fewer
11. less
12. more

Page 42

1. many
2. All
3. No
4. plenty of
5. Each
6. enough
7. several
8. all
9. No
10. each
11. many
12. enough

Page 43

1. less
2. more
3. plenty of
4. Every
5. enough
6. more
7. every
8. a few
9. All
10. plenty

Page 44

1. wrote
2. painted
3. twisted
4. weave
5. knits
6. stretched
7. tie
8. learned
9. made
10. wished

Page 45

1. hopped
2. lounged
3. pounded
4. slurped
5. sewed
6. galloped
7. gulped
8. dragged

Accept all reasonable answers.

Page 46

1. circled
2. watched
3. think
4. train
5. read
6. hunted
7. plunged
8. sculpted
9. spread
10. galloped

Page 47

1. Underline: Tucker; Circle: lives
2. Underline: It; Circle: opens
3. Underline: Tucker; Circle: collected
4. Underline: mouse; Circle: filled
5. Underline: Tucker; Circle: sits
6. Underline: He; Circle: watches
7. Underline: crowd; Circle: passes (singular)
8. Underline: Trains; Circle: run (plural)
9. Underline: Papa; Circle: waits (singular)
10. Underline: station; Circle: feels (singular)
11. Underline: People; Circle: rush (plural)
12. Underline: Mama and Papa; Circle: make (plural)

Page 48

1. make
2. produce
3. listen
4. hear
5. finds
6. calls

7. Mario, wanted; Mario wants the cricket for a pet.
8. He, wished; He wishes for a pet of his own.
9. Crickets, seemed; Crickets seem like unusual pets to his mother.
10. insects, scared; Maybe insects scare her!

Page 49

1. sees
2. surprises
3. catch
4. longs
5. seems
6. correct as is
7. are
8. correct as is
9. viewed
10. experienced

Page 50

1. the, an, the
2. a, an
3. a
4. a
5. the
6. An, the
7. the
8. the, a
9. the
10. a
11. a
12. the
13. a
14. an, a
15. the / an

Page 51

1. Pandas are ~~the~~ rare members of the bear family.
2. They live in bamboo forests in ~~a~~ western China.
3. Pandas eat ~~the~~ nothing but bamboo.
4. They have a black and ~~a~~ white fur coat.
5. They are ~~the~~ excellent tree climbers.
6. ~~The~~ children all over the world adore the panda.
7. A newborn panda is the size of a stick of ~~a~~ butter.
8. It can grow up to ~~the~~ 330 pounds as an adult.
9. In ~~the~~ China, the panda is a national treasure.
10. These cuddly bears are on the edge of ~~an~~ extinction.
11. A group of about 30 people visited <u>the</u> Singapore zoo early one morning
12. They were there to see <u>the</u> pandas Kai Kai and Jia Jia.
13. <u>A</u> long queue started forming at 8 in <u>the</u> morning.
14. <u>The</u> early birds wanted to beat <u>the</u> crowd.
15. One of these was Ken, who said he was <u>an</u> animal lover.
16. You can see the pandas at <u>the</u> Giant Panda Forest, <u>a</u> new tourist attraction.

Page 52

1. no article
2. a
3. the
4. the
5. no article
6. An
7. The/An
8. a
9. the
10. the

Page 53

1. may
2. must
3. can
4. may
5. must
6. can
7. should
8. can
9. may
10. can
11. should

© 2013 Scholastic Education International (S) Pte Ltd ISBN 978-981-07-5259-0

Page 54
1. (a) 1   (b) 2   (c) 3
2. (a) 3   (b) 2   (c) 1
3. (a) 3   (b) 1   (c) 2

Accept all reasonable answers.

Page 55
1. may not   2. must   3. must
4. may   5. can   6. should
7. must   8. may   9. might
10. will

Page 56
1. Underline: Would; Circle: like
2. Underline: May; Circle: get
3. Underline: could; Circle: switch
4. Underline: can; Circle: do
5. Underline: Could; Circle: show
6. Underline: May; Circle: have
7. Underline: Can; Circle: help
8. Underline: Shall; Circle: go
9. Underline: could; Circle: try

Accept all reasonable answers.

Page 57
1. ought to   2. has to   3. ought to
4. needs to   5. ought to   6. have to
7. You ought not to spend time on your Math.
8. James need not ask Ms Peters for help.
9. She ought not to give him extra lessons in Math.

Page 58
1. ought to   2. May   3. Would
4. could   5. Shall   6. Could
7. ought to   8. need not   9. Would
10. could

Page 59
1. Underline: herself; Circle: Ellen
2. Underline: himself; Circle: referee
3. Underline: herself; Circle: Ellen
4. Underline: themselves; Circle: team
5. Underline: themselves; Circle: They
6. Underline: ourselves; Circle: We
7. Underline: herself; Circle: Ellen
8. yourselves   9. ourselves   10. herself
11. themselves   12. himself   13. myself

Page 60
1. Underline: himself; Circle: principal
2. Underline: ourselves; Circle: We
3. Underline: themselves; Circle: girls
4. Underline: herself; Circle: sister
5. Underline: myself; Circle: I
6. Underline: yourself; Circle: You

7. Underline: itself; Circle: concert
Accept all reasonable answers for Questions 8–12.

Page 61
1. You   2. Dad   3. Grandpa
4. Whiskers   5. Mom   6. yourself
7. himself   8. itself   9. themselves
10. myself

Page 62
1. Underline: colorful, dark; Circle: many
2. Underline: small; Circle: A few
3. Underline: strange, unusual; Circle: one
4. Underline: mysterious
5. Underline: big, dark; Circle: four
6. Underline: rare, new
7. Underline: tiny, large, cold
8. Underline: amazing; Circle: several

Accept all reasonable answers.

Page 63
Accept all reasonable answers for Questions 1–5.
6. gray, shaggy, dark   7. some, droopy
8. little, quiet   9. soft, shady
10. enormous, large

Accept all reasonable answers for Questions 11–12.

Page 64
Accept all reasonable answers for Questions 1–5.
6. important   7. suitable   8. two
9. noisy   10. saltwater

Page 65
1. Underline: large, blue plastic; Circle: suitcase
2. Underline: little old luggage; Circle: shop
3. Underline: small, white cardboard; Circle: boxes
4. Underline: expensive, colorful postage; Circle: stamps
5. Underline: kind, elderly maternal; Circle: uncle
6. Underline: elegant, large collector's; Circle: album
7. I saw many types of beautiful, colorful tropical fish.
8. Some tanks were boring, large, rectangular glass containers.
9. Others were modern, round fiberglass tanks.

Page 66
Accept all reasonable answers.

Page 67
1. juicy, large, round cherry
2. worn-out, brown plastic
3. crooked, yellow front

124

4. fresh, green French
5. large, ancient bamboo
6. huge, modern budget

Page 68
1. older
2. loudest
3. higher
4. softer
5. brightest
6. saddest
7. hottest; more than two
8. warmer; two
9. tallest; more than two
10. longer; two
11. friendliest; more than two
12. younger; two

Page 69
1. funniest
2. funnier
3. busier
4. busiest
5. more exciting
6. most exciting
7. more challenging
8. most challenging
9. more tiring
10. most tiring
11. more delicious
12. most delicious

Page 70
1. friendlier
2. most intelligent
3. most graceful
4. more fascinating
5. more dangerous
6. most beautiful
7. swifter
8. noisier
9. more playful
10. largest

Page 71
1. Underline: thing; Circle: day
2. Underline: person; Circle: Dad and Mom
3. Underline: thing; Circle: His start
4. Underline: person; Circle: Jose
5. Underline: thing; Circle: pace
6. Underline: person; Circle: coach
7. Underline: thing; Circle: speed
8. Underline: person; Circle: We
Accept all reasonable answers.

Page 72
1. boring
2. bored
3. annoyed
4. interesting
5. disappointed
6. fascinating
7. surprised
8. embarrassed
9. amusing
10. disgusted
11. concerned
12. encouraging

Page 73
1. Faizal
2. questions
3. Faizal
4. He
5. subject
6. entertaining
7. amusing
8. challenging
9. encouraging
10. amazed

Page 74
1. bought
2. made
3. came
4. rode
5. shook
6. heard

7. took
8. heard
9. made
10. bought
11. broke
12. thought

Page 75
1. have chosen
2. has brought
3. have eaten
4. has hidden
5. had taken
6. have gone
7. had heard
8. have ridden
9. heard
10. taken
11. gone
12. ridden
13. chosen
14. brought

Page 76
1. heard
2. rode
3. stood
4. bought
5. ate
6. has stood
7. have ridden
8. had drawn
9. have kept
10. has taken

Page 77
1. past
2. past
3. future
4. future
5. past
6. present
7. past
8. past
Accept all reasonable answers.

Page 78
1. wears
2. stepped
3. are
4. hurt
5. will buy
6. wants
Accept all reasonable answers.

Page 79
1. future
2. past
3. future
4. present
5. future
6. will begin
7. correct as is
8. will show
9. will perform
10. correct as is

Page 80
1. was raining
2. was making
3. was looking
4. was helping
5. was cooking
6. were not arguing
7. were working
8. was planning
9. was playing
10. was trying
11. was shining
12. was rolling
13. was beginning
14. were cheering

Page 81
1. Underline: was rushing; Circle: heard
2. Underline: was reaching; Circle: came
3. Underline: was stepping; Circle: dashed
4. Underline: was looking; Circle: sounded
5. Underline: was picking; Circle: cut
6. was cheering
7. was playing
8. was feeling
9. were entertaining
10. was crying

Page 82
1. were going
2. was selling
3. was trying
4. were scaring

125

© 2013 Scholastic Education International (S) Pte Ltd ISBN 978-981-07-5259-0

5. was blaring
Accept all reasonable answers.

Page 83
1. Underline: will; Circle: arrive
2. Underline: has; Circle: baked
3. Underline: was; Circle: cleaning
4. Underline: had; Circle: repaired
5. Underline: were; Circle: setting
6. Underline: had ; Circle: asked (past)
7. Underline: will; Circle: drop (future)
8. Underline: is; Circle: learning (present)
9. Underline: will; Circle: enjoy (future)
10. Underline: has; Circle: eaten (past)

Page 84
1. was cooking   2. had added   3. have prepared
4. is tasting   5. will add   6. have arrived
Accept all reasonable answers.

Page 85
1. will travel   2. will photograph
3. had discovered   4. have visited
5. were looking   6. were wondering
7. Underline: will; Write: bake
8. Underline: has; Write: picked
9. Underline: is; Write: picking
10. Underline: had; Circle: planted
11. Underline: have; Circle: tossed
12. Underline: are; Circle: planning

Page 86
1. Jess wanted to go to the circus (and) the theme park.
2. Dad declared it would not be possible to visit the circus (as well as) the theme park.
3. He said it was (not only) too expensive (but also) too time-consuming.
4. At either place, they would have to pay a lot for admission. The food there would be costly, (too.)
5. (Both) Dad (and) Mom agreed that Jess had to choose one or the other.
6. Both the elephants and horses were led into the ring by their trainers.
7. The crowd loved the monkeys as well as the clowns.
8. The flying trapeze act was not only thrilling, but also entertaining.

Page 87
1. but   2. Although   3. while
4. though   5. yet
6. Although the toad and frog are both amphibians, they are different in many ways.
7. Frogs have long hind legs for leaping, but toads have short hind legs for walking.

8. Frogs have smooth or slimy skin while the skin of toads is warty and dry.
9. Frogs tend to lay eggs in clusters though toads tend to lay eggs in long chains.

Page 88
1. yet   2. but
3. not only...but also   4. Although
5. However   6. a motorcycle
7. Ali rides the motorcycle to work
8. but it is also safer
9. it is useful in heavy traffic

Page 89
1. when   2. Before   3. until
4. After   5. as   6. While
7. As soon as   8. As soon as   9. When
10. before   11. after   12. While

Page 90
1. First   2. Then   3. Next   4. As
5. When   6. Then   7. After that
Order should be: 4, 1, 5, 3, 2

Page 91
1. Before   2. First   3. While
4. After   5. Next   6. as
7. after   8. First   9. Then / Next
10. Then / Finally

Page 92
1. Underline: shouted; Circle: Later
2. Underline: hit; Circle: That night
3. Underline: plow; Circle: earlier
4. Underline: went; Circle: Then
5. Underline: fell; Circle: everywhere
6. Underline: trapped; Circle: inside
7. Underline: tunneled; Circle: from
8. Underline: built; Circle: by
9. Underline: never (when)
10. Underline: underground (where)
11. Underline: inside (where)
12. Underline: Soon (when)

Page 93
1. Underline: talked; Circle: happily
2. Underline: squawked; Circle: sharply
3. Underline: greeted; Circle: warmly
4. Underline: guided; Circle: expertly
5. Underline: recorded; Circle: faithfully
6. Underline: looked; Circle: eagerly
7. Underline: jumped; Circle: quickly
8. Underline: snorkeled; Circle: easily

126

9. Underline: saw; Circle: clearly
10. Underline: gazed; Circle: intently
11. Underline: surrounded; Circle: Swiftly
Accept all reasonable answers.

Page 94
1. rapidly   2. loudly   3. strong
4. somewhat   5. quickly   6. swam
7. curious   8. One   9. nudged
10. disappeared

Page 95
1. Underline: Yesterday   2. Circle: monthly
3. Circle: daily   4. Circle: Usually
5. Circle: Occasionally   6. Circle: never
7. Circle: Sometimes   8. Circle: always
9. always   10. daily
11. Sometimes   12. usually
13. monthly

Page 96
1. Underline: often; Circle: travels
2. Underline: usually, sometimes; Circle: goes
3. Underline: monthly; Circle: makes
4. Underline: seldom; Circle: comes
5. Underline: always; Circle: like
6. Underline: Yesterday; Circle: gave
7. Underline: immediately; Circle: ran
8. Underline: Early; Circle: left
9. Underline: soon; Circle: bring
10. Underline: seldom; Circle: disappoints
11. yesterday   12. seldom   13. often

Page 97
1. works   2. misses   3. jogs
4. joins   5. stops   6. tonight
7. seldom   8. temporarily   9. always

Page 98
1. feel   2. get   3. take
4. take   5. have   6. have
7. stay   8. visit   9. get
10. be   11. put   12. work
13. tell   14. be   15. make

Page 99
1. to buy   2. to prepare   3. to cook
4. to order   5. to teach, to choose
6. to watch   7. to eat
8. to watch, to take   9. arrive
10. celebrate   11. see   12. start

Page 100
1. watch   2. get   3. see
4. know   5. explain   6. look

7. see   8. light   9. follow
10. watch

Page 101
1. She'll → She will   2. You'd → You had
3. doesn't → does not   4. Don't → Do not
5. You're → You are   6. I'll → I will / I shall
7. aren't → are not   8. wouldn't → would not
9. shan't → shall not   10. won't → will not
11. we'll → we will   12. it's → it is

Page 102
1. They're   2. I'll   3. isn't
4. he'd   5. I'm   6. You're
Accept all reasonable answers.

Page 103
1. They'll   2. mustn't   3. you've
4. We've   5. It's   6. isn't
7. She's   8. She'll   9. I'm
10. mustn't

Page 104
1. "I am a big fan of hers," replied Sharon.
2. I added, "Sally can even sing a wolf to sleep."
3. "How did Sally tame King Bear?" asked our teacher.
4. "Sally ought to be in the movies," said Don.
5. "What kind of person is Sally?" asked Davy.
6. The man replied, "Sally is a special friend."
7. "She can laugh the bark off a tree," added Lucy.
8. The man said, "She can dance a rock to pieces."
9. "I'm very impressed!" exclaimed Davy.
Accept all reasonable answers.

Page 105
1. "Well, we are having a food drive next week."
2. "Oh, Ed, can you bring some containers to school?"
3. "Yes, I have several at home, Jody."
4. "Thank you, Mr Poole, for all your suggestions."
5. "Kim, your posters for the talent contest are terrific!" I exclaimed.
6. She replied, "Thank you."
7. Our teacher asked, "Meg, will you play your guitar or sing?"
8. "Oh, I plan to do both, "said Meg.
9. "Will you be juggling this year, Robert?" Jay asked.
10. "No, I want to do a comedy routine," he replied.
Accept all reasonable answers.

Page 106
1. "Rosa, tell me a joke," said Ken.
2. "What years do frogs like best?" asked Rosa.
3. "Frogs like Hoppy New Years!" laughed Ken.
4. "No, frogs like leap years," said Rosa.

© 2013 Scholastic Education International (S) Pte Ltd   ISBN 978-981-07-5259-0

5. "Oh, that was funny!" exclaimed Ken.
6. "I like your joke too," said Rosa.
7. "Do you have any more jokes?" asked Ken.

Page 107
1. loves, loved   2. likes, liked   3. we, they
4. We, They
5. Tracy said she could buy the ice cream on her way to Tom's house.
6. Hakim added that he would bring the birthday card along.
7. Judy said that she was sure he would have a pleasant surprise.

Page 108
1. "I went to France last year," Grace told me.
   Grace told me that she had gone to France the previous year.
2. "I can still remember how many steps we climbed to get to the top of the Eiffel Tower," she said.
   She said that she could still remember how many steps they had climbed to get to the top of the Eiffel Tower.
3. "What I really loved were the desserts," she added.
   She added that what she had really loved had been the desserts.
4. Miss Henny told the girls that she had asked them to discuss their vacation plans for that summer.
5. She added that she had not told them to talk about what they had done the previous summer.

Page 109
1. We   2. has   3. last   4. is   5. I
6. We → They   7. I → She   8. can → could
9. did → had   10. are → was

Page 110
1. into, on   2. around   3. above
4. against   5. behind   6. outside
7. along   8. between   9. past
10. on   11. in   12. over

Page 111
1. during, time   2. when, time
3. beside, position   4. behind, position
5. for, time   6. near

7. for   8. among
9. above   10. before

Page 112
1. in   2. in   3. After
4. during   5. along   6. on
7. behind   8. on   9. Underneath
10. over

Page 113
1. from   2. across   3. from, towards
4. over   5. through   6. past
Accept all reasonable answers.

Page 114
1. through   2. out of   3. past
4. from   5. towards   6. into
7. over   8. around
Accept all reasonable answers.

Page 115
1. between   2. under   3. across
4. through   5. over   6. along
7. towards   8. into   9. onto
10. past

Pages 116–119
1. proper noun   2. common noun
3. common noun   4. collective noun
5. they   6. him
7. himself   8. them
9. no   10. a
11. a few   12. all
13. thought   14. found
15. become   16. has found
17. may   18. might
19. look   20. lovely
21. more beautiful   22. worst
23. big, golden round   24. depressed
25. small wise old   26. powerful
27. soon   28. hurriedly
29. Usually   30. sadly
31. never   32. because
33. Although   34. because
35. so   36. while

© 2013 Scholastic Education International (S) Pte Ltd ISBN 978-981-07-5259-0